A History of
Pan-African Revolt

A History of Pan-African Revolt

C.L.R. JAMES

INTRODUCTION BY ROBIN D.G. KELLEY

MERLIN

A *History of Pan-African Revolt*
C.L.R. James

This edition ©2012 PM Press

ISBN: 978-1-60486-095-5
LCCN: 2011939689

Cover and interior design: Antumbra Design/Antumbradesign.org

10 9 8 7 6 5 4 3

PM Press
PO Box 23912
Oakland, CA 94623
www.pmpress.org

Published in conjunction with the Charles H. Kerr Publishing
Company
C.H. Kerr Company
1726 Jarvis Avenue
Chicago, IL 60626
www.charleshkerr.com

Printed in the USA on recycled paper by the Employee Owners of
Thomson-Shore in Dexter, Michigan. www.thomsonshore.com

Contents

Publisher's Foreword

(1995)

It is a real honor and pleasure for the Charles H. Kerr Publishing Company to bring out a new edition of this classic work by the great revolutionary historian, theorist and activist C.L.R. James. Originally issued in England in 1938, and expanded in 1969, the book has heretofore circulated almost in "underground" fashion. Hopefully this new Charles H. Kerr edition will help bring it the wider attention it very much deserves.

When Comrade James gave us permission to reissue two of his out-of-print works, it was his intention to write a new foreword for each. To the reissue of *State Capitalism and World Revolution* he contributed a foreword titled "Fully and Absolutely Assured," which, despite its brevity, is an important

amplification of his views. We sharply regret that our own finan-
cially driven delays in publication and C.L.R.'s 1989 death cause
this edition to appear without such a foreword.

Fortunately, however, this new edition features a valuable
introduction by Robin D.G. Kelley, Professor of History and
Africana Studies at New York University. Author of *Hammer and
Hoe: Alabama Communists in the Great Depression* (University
of North Carolina Press, 1990) and *Race Rebels: Culture, Politics,
and the Black Working Class* (Free Press, 1994), and co-author
(with Sidney Lemelle) of *Imagining Home: Class, Culture, and
Nationalism in the African Diaspora* (Verso, 1995), Kelley is a
rare modern scholar whose breadth, clarity, and vision call James
to mind.

In his introduction Kelley discusses the book's previous publishers: the Independent Labour Party journal *FACT*, the short-
lived Drum and Spear Press of Washington, D.C., and the *Race
Today* collective in London. This seems to be an appropriate place
to acquaint readers with the publishers of the current edition.

Founded in Chicago in 1886, a few weeks prior to the police riot at Haymarket Square, the Charles H. Kerr Company
in less than a decade developed into the principal publisher of
radical books and pamphlets in the United States. By 1900, the
Kerr Company had rallied to the banner of international working
class socialism. Through the first quarter of the twentieth century, "that struggling socialist publishing house in Chicago," as
Jack London called it in *The Iron Heel*, was the largest publisher
of revolutionary literature in the English-speaking world.

Publication of the revolutionary classics was an early Kerr
Company priority, and it has remained so ever since. In the years
1906–1909 Kerr brought out, for the first time in English, the
three volumes of Karl Marx's *Capital*, and also published many
other works by Marx and his co-thinker, Friedrich Engels. The
Kerr Company's standard edition of the *Communist Manifesto*
has been continuously in print, through countless editions, since
1902. Antonio Labriola, Paul Lafargue, Eugene V. Debs, James
Connolly, Peter Kropotkin, Edward Bellamy, William Morris,
"Mother" Jones, William D. Haywood, Sen Katayama, Louis B.
Boudin, Mary E. Marcy, and Austin Lewis are only a few of the

many important revolutionary writers whose works were made available by Charles H. Kerr.

The Great Depression and the Cold War were an exceptionally difficult period for America's pioneer working class publishing house, but somehow the fellow workers who kept it going managed to keep a good number of the socialist classics in print. When Fred Thompson and others helped get the cooperative back on its feet in the early 1970s, the Board of Directors resolved to do their best to reissue the out-of-print classics and, insofar as limited finances allow, to add new ones to the list.

A Note on the Text

Apart from Americanizing the spelling (labor instead of labour, maneuver rather than manoeuvre, today without a hyphen, etc.), and making a few minor corrections, the text of this edition follows that of its predecessors. Only twice have we dared to change a word. Writing for readers in the British Isles, James once (on page 63 of this edition) refers in passing to America's Parliament; to avoid confusion, we have substituted Congress.

The second change appears in the Epilogue. James's Epilogue was dictated, not written, and in the course of transcription part of a sentence was omitted in the Drum and Spear Press edition, and was not corrected in the *Race Today* edition. Since no manuscript of this text exists, and the present location of the tape-recording of it is unknown, we have taken the liberty of attempting to fill in the missing words to make the sentence comprehensible.

Introduction

Should world events give these people a chance, they will destroy what has them by the throat as surely as the San Domingo blacks destroyed the French plantocracy.
—C.L.R. James[1]

I

We are all indebted to the Charles H. Kerr Publishing Company for re-issuing C.L.R. James's important but little-known book, *A History of Pan-African Revolt*. Originally published in 1938 under the title *A History of Negro Revolt*, this brief but highly suggestive global history of black

1. *A History of Pan-African Revolt*, 103. I am deeply grateful to Franklin Rosemont and David Roediger for inviting me to write a new introduction for *A History of Pan-African Revolt*, to Scott McLemee for sharing some of his research with me; to James Early for taking time out of his busy schedule to track down members of the original "Drum and Spear" Collective; to Charlie Cobb for providing valuable information about how Drum and Spear brought this book back into print in 1969; and to Paul Buhle, Robert Hill, and Cedric Robinson for their mentorship over the years—particularly with respect to James's life and thought.

resistance appeared the same year as James's magnum opus, *The Black Jacobins: Toussaint L'Ouverture and the San Domingo Revolution,* and thus lived in its shadow ever since. Although it was brought back into print with a new epilogue by James in 1969, and again in 1985, by small activist publishing outlets, *A History of Pan-African Revolt*—as the later editions were titled—has remained one of the best kept secrets among a handful of Marxists and black militants. It never sold many copies, but everyone familiar with James's ideas or the resurgence of Pan-Africanism in the 1960s knew of its influence. The late Walter Rodney, the great historian and Guyanese revolutionary, once called it "a mine of ideas advancing far ahead of its time."[2]

Ahead of its time, indeed. Five years before the publication of Herbert Aptheker's *American Negro Slave Revolts* and just three years after the appearance of W.E.B. DuBois's *Black Reconstruction in America* (another book way, way ahead of its time), *A History of Negro Revolt* excoriated imperialism and placed black laborers at the center of world events when the leading historians of his day believed Africans were savages, colonialism was a civilizing mission, and slavery was a somewhat benevolent institution. James knew he was challenging established fictions. "The only place where Negroes did not revolt," he wrote in 1939, "is in the pages of capitalist historians."[3] He had set out to tell the story of the so-called "inarticulate" masses in motion, of black workers and peasants fighting their European masters, of an ambivalent black petite-bourgeoisie whose stand vis-à-vis capitalism and colonial domination was never certain. By broadly defining black workers as all who labor or whom colonial powers hope to turn into cheap wage

---

2. Walter Rodney, "The African Revolution" in *C.L.R. James: His Life and Work,* ed. Paul Buhle, special issue of *Urgent Tasks* 12 (Summer 1981): 5.

3. James, "Revolution and the Negro," reprinted in *C.L.R. James and Revolutionary Marxism: Selected Writings of C.L.R. James, 1939–1949,* eds. Scott McLemee and Paul LeBlanc (Atlantic Highlands: Humanities Press International, 1994), 77. The essay is essentially a synopsis of *A History of Negro Revolt* written under the name J.R. Johnson for the *New International* (December 1939).

slaves or market-driven peasants, James casts his net widely and includes slave revolts, strikes, millenarian movements, and a vast array of anti-racist protests.

As a study of "Negro" rebellions, *A History of Negro Revolt* completely revised African and diasporic history by focusing on the masses. Of course, there are leaders, but like Toussaint L'Ouverture in San Domingo, leaders are made by the masses and the times in which they live. James makes a point of describing how the masses defend their leaders by freeing them from jail cells, hiding them in huts and cellars, pummeling their detractors into silence. It is the masses, and only the masses, that can make the Utopian speeches of a Simon Kimbangu, a John Chilembwe, a Marcus Garvey, or a Kwame Nkrumah a reality.

A History of Negro Revolt, however, was not simply an outgrowth of James's vision and brilliance. It was a collective endeavor, a product of specific political campaigns, debates and intellectual exchange with some of the leading black radical thinkers of the twentieth century. It is not just another history book; it is a historical document in its own right, a testament to the streams of radical thought that converged in London's cafes, libraries, and underheated flats where young Africans and West Indians gathered during the 1930s—the decade when fascism and a depressed economy threw into question the fate of humanity.

II

Cyril Lionel Robert James was barely in his thirties when he began circulating among London's black radicals. And given his background, living the life of a Marxist intellectual with Pan-Africanist leanings was hardly what he or his parents had in mind. The son of a school teacher born in the small village of Tunapuna, Trinidad, in 1901, James was raised solidly middle class—at least in terms of cultural capital if not actual money. He read Thackeray and Shakespeare with enthusiasm, and due to his mother's influence he became an inveterate reader of history, literature, and to a lesser degree politics. He refused to stay within the boundaries of bourgeois culture, however. He adored

Carnival, calypso, and jazz, despite his Puritan mom's warnings, and he deeply loved the game of cricket. After earning a school certificate from Queen's Royal College in 1918, he decided to stay in Trinidad and become a school master. In his spare time he wrote and lectured on many topics, including calypso and cricket, and soon developed a reputation throughout the island as a brilliant young scholar with intelligent things to say about Caribbean popular culture. He was drawn to nationalist politics when Captain Arthur Cipriani, the celebrated Trinidadian labor leader of French Creole heritage, asked him to write articles on cricket and assorted cultural and political issues for the *Socialist*, the organ of the Trinidad Workingmen's Association (TWA). James went on to write a pamphlet titled *The Life of Captain Cipriani: An Account of British Government in the West Indies*, which was published in Trinidad in 1932. (An abridged version appeared a year later in England under the title *The Case for West Indian Self Government*). While the pamphlet and his work with the *Socialist* represents an early stage in James's politicization, he was still a long way from the militant anti-imperialist he would eventually become. Never an activist for the TWA, James identified with the Labour Party and firmly believed in parliamentary politics.[4]

But England changed all that. In 1932, James left his homeland to assist Sir Learie Constantine, the great West Indian cricketer turned lawyer, write a book on cricket and English society.[5] To make ends meet, James took a job as a cricket correspondent for the *Manchester Guardian* and settled down in Lancashire. It was in Lancashire that he began his rapid drift to the left. His discussions with local workers made him more critical of capi-

---

4. On James's early life, see Paul Buhle, *C.L.R. James: The Artist as Revolutionary* (London: Verso, 1988), 7–37; *C.L.R. James, Beyond a Boundary* (Durham, NC: Duke University Press, 1993), 4–46; Robert A. Hill, "In England, 1932–1938," in *C.L.R. James: His Life and Work*, ed. Paul Buhle (London: Verso, 1988), 19–22; Anna Grimshaw, ed., *The C.L.R. James Reader* (Oxford: Blackwell, 1992), 4–5; Kent Worcester, *C.L.R. James: A Political Biography* (Oxford: Blackwell, 1993).

5. Constantine's book was published a year later under the title *Cricket and I* (London: Allan, 1933).

talism and compelled him to study the "classics" of Marxism, including the book that would have a profound impact on his conception of history: Leon Trotsky's three-volume *History of the Russian Revolution*. After relocating to London, he found his way into the Trotskyist camp and soon emerged as one of its main spokespersons. Indeed, by 1937 he had published a major book titled *World Revolution, 1917–1936: The Rise and Fall of the Communist International*, which happened to be the first Trotskyist history of the Comintern ever published.[6]

Thus it was as a budding Trotskyist and supporter of the Independent Labour Party that James entered London's hotbed of black anti-colonial and Pan-Africanist politics. They came from different colonies and different ideological camps, but they all shared a patriotic love for the Motherland and her wayward children. Some, like Egyptian Duse Mohammed Ali, veteran Pan-Africanist and founder of the *African Times and Orient Review*, were longtime residents of London. Others, such as Sierra Leonean radical I.T.A. Wallace Johnson, Kenya's future president Jomo Kenyatta, and the Guyanese-born T. Ras Makonnen (born George Thomas Nathaniel Griffith) were—like James—fairly recent newcomers. These young intellectuals did more than talk; they formed a variety of political organizations and associations in London and throughout Europe, including the West African Students Association, the Ethiopian Progressive Association, and the League of Coloured Peoples founded by Jamaican physician Harold Moody.[7]

One of the most important men among these circles turned out to be James's childhood friend Malcolm Nurse. Now known

6. Cedric J. Robinson, *Black Marxism: The Making of the Black Radical Tradition* (London: Zed Press, 1983), 375; Buhle, *C.L.R. James*, 44–52; "In England, 1932–1938," 22–23.

7. P. Olisanwuche Esedebe, *Pan-Africanism: The Idea and Movement, 1776–1963* (Washington, DC: Howard University Press, 1982), 66; A. Adu Boahen, "Politics and Nationalism in West Africa, 1919–1935," in *General History of Africa, Vol. VII: Africa Under Colonial Domination, 1880–1935*, ed. Boahen (London: Heinemann Educational Books, 1985), 629; Immanuel Geiss, *The Pan-African Movement* (London: Methuen and Co., 1974), 730; Robinson, *Black Marxism*, 370.

as "George Padmore," he had become a leading figure in the international Communist movement. He left Trinidad for the United States as a young man and joined the Communist Party almost as soon as he stepped off the boat in New York Harbor. A militant organizer while at Howard University in Washington, D.C., Padmore rose quickly within the Communist ranks and was eventually sent to study in the Soviet Union. So popular was he that the citizens of Moscow elected him to the City Council! As a student at the University of the Toilers of the East, he could have run into any number of African leaders who, like him, had been drawn to the Communist camp. Among the more prominent students were I.T.A. Wallace Johnson, Jomo Kenyatta, and South African Communists Moses Kotane, Edwin Mofutsanyana and Albert Nzula.[8]

The impressive gathering of black radicals in Moscow not only contributed to the development of a left-wing Pan-Africanism but probably shaped Padmore's vision of a black international working class movement that could unite Africa and the diaspora in a coordinated effort to overthrow colonialism, racism, and ultimately capitalism.

Thus, when he became secretary of the International Trade Union Council of Negro Workers (ITUC-NW) and editor of its journal, *Negro Worker*, Padmore saw no conflict between his work on behalf of African liberation and the struggle for socialism. In Padmore's view the ITUC-NW (which he first directed from Hamburg until it was forced to move to Copenhagen and then Paris) was much more than the black arm of the Red International of Labor Unions (Prointern); it was the vanguard in the struggle for worldwide black liberation. Unfortunately, Padmore's hopes for the ITUC-NW were dashed almost as soon

---

8. James R. Hooker, *Black Revolutionary: George Padmore's Path from Communism to Pan-Africanism* (New York: Praeger, 1967), 10–37; Boahen, "Politics and Nationalism in West Africa," 629; L. Rytov, "Ivan Potekhin: A Great Africanist," *African Communist* 54 (Third Quarter, 1973), 95; Brian Bunting, *Moses Kotane: South African Revolutionary* (London: Inkululeko Publications, 1975), 58–59; Edward T. Wilson, *Russia and Black Africa Before World War II* (New York and London: Holmes & Meier, 1974).

as it got off the ground. By the time Padmore became James's political ally in 1935, he no longer believed that the Communist International could play a progressive role in the African liberation movement. With the transition to the Popular Front, the Comintern made fascism its main priority and put anti-colonial movements on the back burner.[9]

In retrospect, perhaps Padmore should have seen it coming. But in 1930, he had good reason to believe in the Comintern's commitment, if not their sincerity, to the emancipation of Africans and people of African descent. As early as 1922, the Fourth Congress of the Comintern adopted a set of theses describing blacks as a nationality oppressed by worldwide imperialist exploitation. Because black workers' struggles were now thought to be inherently anti-imperialist, Communists were obliged to view black nationalist and anti-colonial movements more sympathetically. Moreover, the "Theses" recognized the success of the UNIA under Marcus Garvey, as well as the Pan-African Congresses led by W.E.B. DuBois, and urged that immediate steps be taken by the Comintern to call a world congress of African leaders.[10] The Comintern did more than appropriate

---

9. Hooker, *Black Revolutionary*, 36–37; C.L.R. James, "Notes on the Life of George Padmore," in *The C.L.R. James Reader*, 288–95; C.L.R. James, "George Padmore: Black Marxist Revolutionary," in *At the Rendezvous of Victory* (London: Allison & Busby, 1984).

10. Theodore Draper, *American Communism and Soviet Russia* (New York: Viking Press, 1960), 320–21, 327–28; Robinson, *Black Marxism*, 304; Roger E. Kanet, "The Comintern and the 'Negro Question': Communist Policy in the United States and Africa, 1921–1941," *Survey* 19, no. 4 (Autumn 1973): 89–90; Harry Haywood, *Black Bolshevik: Autobiography of an Afro-American Communist* (Chicago: Liberator Press, 1978), 225; Claude McKay, *A Long Way From Home* (New York: Lee Furman, 1937), 177–80; Billings [Otto Huiswoud], "Report on the Negro Question," *International Press Correspondence* 3, no. 2 (1923): 14–16. The full text of the "Theses on the Negro (Question" is available in *Bulletin of the IV Congress of the Communist International* 17 (December 7, 1922): 8–10. The Fourth Congress was significant, but one might go back to the debates between V.I. Lenin and Indian Communist M.N. Roy over the anti-colonial movement and the right of oppressed minorities to self-determination. V.I. Lenin, "The Socialist Revolution and the Right of Nations to Self-Determination (Theses),"

the familiar idioms of Pan-Africanism; during the late 1920s and early 1930s it actively supported anti-colonial movements. In 1926, for example, leading members of the German Communist Party founded the League Against Colonial Oppression to combat pro-colonial sentiments emerging in Germany. After a successful international conference in Brussels in 1927, it became clear to those in attendance that the League marked an important step toward coordinating various struggles for national liberation in the colonies and "semi-colonies," and it served as an intermediary between the Communist International and the anticolonial movement. The conferees, among them Jomo Kenyatta and Jawaharlal Nehru, passed a general resolution that proclaimed: "Africa for the Africans, and their full freedom and equality with other races and the right to govern Africa."[11]

The Sixth World Congress of the Comintern in 1928 passed an even more explicit resolution asserting that African Americans in the U.S. South and Africans under white domination in South Africa constituted oppressed nations and thus possessed an inherent right of self-determination. For many black Communists in Africa, the United States, and even the West Indies, the resolution on black self-determination indi-

---

in *Lenin on the National and Colonial Questions: Three Articles* (Peking: Foreign Language Press, 1967), 5; "Theses on the National and Colonial Question Adopted by the Second Congress of the Comintern," in *The Communist International, 1919–1943, Documents*, vol. I, ed. Jane Degras (London: Oxford University Press, 1956), 142. For Lenin's views on Roy's supplementary theses, see "The Report of the Commission on the National and Colonial Questions, July 26, 1920," in *Lenin on the National and Colonial Questions*, 30–37; Draper, American Communism and Soviet Russia, 321.

11. Willy Munzenberg, "Pour une Conference Coloniale," *Correspondance Internationale* 6, no. 9 (August 1926): 1011; Willy Munzenberg, "La Premiere Conference Mondiale Contre la Politique Coloniale Imperialiste," *Correspondance Internationale* 7, no. 17 (February 5, 1927): 232; Robin D.G. Kelley, "The Third International and the Struggle for National Liberation in South Africa, 1921–1928," *Ufahamu* 15, no. 1–2 (1986): 110–11; Edward T. Wilson, *Russia and Black Africa*, 151; *South African Worker*, April 1, June 24, 1927; "Les Decisions du Congres: Resolution Commune sur la Question Negre," *La Voix des Negres* 1, no. 3 (March 1927): 3.

rectly confirmed what they had long believed: black people had their own unique revolutionary tradition. Black Communists published dozens of articles documenting the autonomous traditions of radicalism among Africans and people of African descent. "Aside from the purely Marxian analysis," wrote African American Communist Gilbert Lewis in the pages of the *Negro Worker*, "the Negro's history is replete with many actual instances of uprising against his exploiters and oppressors."[12]

In 1930, Padmore set out to document that history in an important book titled *The Life and Struggles of Negro Toilers*. In some ways it provided a model for James's *A History of Negro Revolt* and inspired other contemporary and historical studies on African workers.[13] Published in 1931 by the Red International of Labor Unions, this 126-page book was written primarily for workers in the Western capitalist countries who failed to comprehend why anti-colonial movements are integral to proletarian emancipation. Although he touches on slavery and pays attention to black resistance, *Life and Struggles* is more descriptive than historical. His primary purpose is to in-

---

12. Mark Naison, *Communists in Harlem During the Depression*, (Urbana: University of Illinois Press, 1983), 18; Gilbert Lewis, "Revolutionary Negro Tradition," *Negro Worker*, March 15, 1930, 8. Cyril Briggs published a whole series of essays on this score, such as "Negro Revolutionary Hero—Toussaint L'Ouverture," *Communist* 8, no. 5 (May 1929): 250–54; "The Negro Press as a Class Weapon," *Communist* 8, no. 8 (August 1929): 453–60; and "May First and the Revolutionary Traditions of Negro Masses," *Daily Worker*, April 28, 1930.

13. The most obvious example is Albert Nzula, I.I. Potekhin, and A.Z. Zusmanovich, *Forced Labour in Colonial Africa*, ed. Robin Cohen (London: Zed Press, 1979). It was originally published in Russian as *Rabochee Dvizhenie i Prinuditel'ni trud V Negrityanskoi Afrike* (Moscow: Profizdat, 1933), which roughly translates as *The Working Class Movement and Forced Labor in Negro Africa*. (Nzula, at the time of publication, was using the pseudonym Tom Jackson.) As historian Robin Cohen notes, "In its scope, ambition and subject-matter, Padmore's book clearly provided a strong inspiration for Nzula, Potekhin and Zusmanovich, though Padmore's subsequent disgrace and expulsion has meant that there are no direct citations from his text by the three authors who only show by occasional allusion, that they are familiar with his work." (Ibid., 15)

dict imperialism by documenting the horrible conditions black workers throughout the world had to endure. In addition to eliciting sympathy for black workers, Padmore wanted to show that the profits generated from the exploitation of colonial labor allowed capitalists "to bribe the reformist and social fascist trade union bureaucrats and thereby enable them to betray the struggles of workers."[14] In the end, however, the role of enlightened white workers—the progressives who had not been bought off—was to educate "backward" black workers of the futility of racial chauvinism and persuade them to cast their lot with the worldwide proletariat. It was a position James would find untenable.

III

As C.L.R. James drifted deeper into the world of Trotskyism, preparing for the Fourth International and cursing Stalinism's betrayal of Lenin's vision, Padmore drifted out of the Communist movement altogether. In 1935 they ended up in the same place, thanks to Italy's invasion of Ethiopia. Indeed, virtually every self-respecting black activist, irrespective of their national origins or ideological bent, joined the Ethiopian defense campaigns. Literally dozens of support organizations were formed throughout the world to raise money for relief and medical aid; and black men from the Caribbean, the United States, and Africa volunteered to fight in Emperor Haile Selassie's army. T. Ras Makonnen, a comrade of James and Padmore in the Ethiopian solidarity movement, recalls the impact the invasion had on the black world: "Letters simply poured into our office from blacks on three continents asking where could they register. . . . And the same was true of Africa. When the Italians entered Addis Ababa, it was reported that school children wept in the Gold Coast."[15]

---

14. George Padmore, *The Life and Struggles of Negro Toilers* (London: The RILU Magazine for the International Trade Union Committee of Negro Workers, 1931), 6.

15. William R. Scott, "Black Nationalism and the Italo-Ethiopian Conflict, 1934–1936," *Journal of Negro History* 63, no. 2 (1978): 121,

The overwhelming response to the invasion should not be surprising, for Ethiopia was not just any African country. Also known as Abyssinia, it held considerable historical, religious, and cultural significance for black people the world over. Not only had the Ethiopians under Emperor Menelik II managed to retain their independence while the rest of Africa was being carved up by Europeans, but their land had developed a reputation as the cradle of civilization, having been among the first countries in the world to adopt Christianity. In the black Christian world, Ethiopia has remained one of its principal icons and, in some ways, might be called an "African Jerusalem." As historian William Scott explained, many African Americans believed that "Ethiopia had been predestined by biblical prophecy to redeem the black race from white rule." Their point of reference, of course, was the biblical passage "Ethiopia shall stretch forth her hands unto God" (Psalm 68:31). The Garvey movement, whose official anthem was entitled "Ethiopia, Thou Land of Our Fathers," made constant reference to this African nation in its songs, rituals, and symbols.[16]

128–29; Naison, *Communists in Harlem*, 138–40; Bernard Makhosezwe Magubane, *The Ties That Bind: African-American Consciousness of Africa* (Trenton, NJ: Africa World Press, 1987), 166–67; Cedric J. Robinson, "The African Diaspora and the Italo-Ethiopian Crisis," *Race and Class* 27, no. 2 (Autumn 1985): 51–65; Robert Weisbord, *Ebony Kinship: Africa, Africans, and the Afro-American* (Westport, CN: Greenwood Press, 1973), 94–100; S.K.B. Asante, "The Afro-American and the Italo-Ethiopian Crisis, 1934–1936," *Race* 15, no. 2 (1973): 167–84; T. Ras Makonnen, *Pan-Africanism Within*, edited Kenneth King (Nairobi and London: Oxford University Press, 1973), 116.

16. Scott, "Black Nationalism and the Italo-Ethiopian Conflict," 118–21; Gayraud Wilmore, *Black Religion and Black Radicalism: An Interpretation of the Religious History of Afro-American People* (Maryknoll, NY: Orbis Books, 2nd ed.), 120–21, 126–28, 160–61; Edward Ullendorff, *Ethiopia and the Bible* (London: Published for the British Academy by Oxford University Press, 1968); W.A. Shack, "Ethiopia and Afro-Americans: Some Historical Notes, 1920–1970," *Phylon* 35, no. 2 (1974): 142–55; Magubane, *The Ties That Bind*, 160–65; S.K.B. Asante, *Pan-African Protest: West Africa and the Italo-Ethiopian Crisis, 1934–1941* (London: Longman, 1977), 9–38; Weisbord, *Ebony Kinship*, 90–92; Randall K. Burkett, *Garveyism as a Religious Movement: The Institutionalization*

For the black Left, however, sentimentality and racial pride clouded the issue at hand: imperialism. While "race" scholars praised Abyssinia for its ancient civilizations, its written language, its rulers' proud claim of direct lineage to Solomon and the Queen of Sheba, black leftists discussed a mountainous peasant region in the Horn of Africa ruled by a dying monarchy that did not believe in land reform. As one of the few regions on earth where slavery persisted well into the early 1930s, Ethiopia was hardly a land of milk and honey. Indeed, in *The Life and Struggles of Negro Toilers*, Padmore characterized Abyssinia as a feudal oligarchy under a reactionary emperor and called for an internal revolution against "the reactionary religious hierarchy and the feudal system."[17]

But before the revolution could take place, they first needed to kick Mussolini's troops out of there. In August of 1935, James formed the International African Friends of Ethiopia.[18] With C.L.R. as chairman, its active members included Padmore, Jomo Kenyatta, I.T.A. Wallace Johnson, Amy Ashwood Garvey (ex-wife of Marcus Garvey), T. Ras Makonnen, and Albert Marryshaw, who had attended the 1921 Pan-African Congress in London. James was the IAFE's most active propagandist, publishing several articles in the *New Leader*, weekly paper of the Independent Labour Party, and one very substantial piece in *The Keys*, the official organ of the League of Coloured People.[19] These articles reveal James groping to reconcile two political

of a Black Civil Religion (Metuchen, NJ: Scarecrow Press, 1978), 34–35, 85–86, 122, 125, 134–35; George Shepperson, "Ethiopianism and African Nationalism," *Phylon* 14, no. 1 (1953): 9–18.

17. Padmore, *Life and Struggles*, 77; on slavery in Ethiopia, see Jon R. Edwards, "Slavery, the Slave Trade and the Economic Reorganization of Ethiopia, 1916–1934," *African Economic History* 11 (1982): 3–14.

18. The original name of the organization was the International African Friends of Abyssinia, or IAFA, but soon after its founding they decided to replace Abyssinia with "Ethiopia."

19. C.L.R. James, "Notes on the Life of George Padmore," 292; Buhle, *C.L.R. James*, 55–56; Esedebe, Pan-Africanism, 115. The essay James published in *The Keys*, "Abyssinia and the Imperialists," was reprinted in *The C.L.R. James Reader*, 63–66.

worlds: Pan-Africanism and socialism. On the one hand, he took the position that the imperialist countries used the defense of Ethiopia as a pretext for war. Yet, as a black man who probably felt a tinge of pride in Ethiopia's legacy, and whose admiration for Africa ran much deeper than anti-imperialism, he felt obligated to defend the place of his ancestors. In his personal struggle to bring these two traditions together, he volunteered for service in the Ethiopian military:

> My reasons for this were simple. International Socialists in Britain fight British Imperialism because obviously it is more convenient to do so than fight, for instance, German Imperialism. But Italian Capitalism is the same enemy, only a little further removed.
>
> My hope was to get into the army. It would have given me an opportunity to make contact not only with the masses of the Abyssinians and other Africans, but in the ranks with them I would have had the best possible opportunity of putting across the International Socialist case. I believed also that I could have been useful in helping to organize anti-Fascist propaganda among the Italian troops. . . .
>
> I did not intend to spend the rest of my life in Abyssinia, but, all things considered, I thought, and still think, that two or three years there, given the fact that I am a Negro and am especially interested in the African revolution, was well worth the attempt.[20]

James, like many others, never had a chance to go. Haile Selassie discouraged volunteers in hopes of securing support from Western democracies and the League of Nations, and as soon as Italy's occupation became an accomplished fact, he and the royal family fled to England.

Soon after the Ethiopian crisis subsided, IAFE members regrouped and formed the International African Service Bureau (IASB) with Padmore at the helm. James edited its monthly journal. *International African Opinion,* from July to October 1938,

---

20 Robinson, *Black Marxism,* 382.

and fed vital information to political organizations and newspapers about the situation in Africa. The IASB set out to keep the issue of colonialism in the public mind—not an easy task given the specter of fascism and the inevitability of war in Europe.[21]

Nevertheless, Ethiopia was the turning point in James's thinking and writing. The events surrounding the invasion and the failure of Western democracies to come to Ethiopia's defense pushed James beyond European Marxism toward a deeper understanding of the traditions of the black resistance. In a review of George Padmore's book, *How Britain Rules Africa* (1936), James lambasted his comrade for suggesting that enlightened sections of the ruling class could play a progressive role in the liberation of Africa from colonial domination. "Africans must win their own freedom," he insisted. "Nobody will win it for them."[22] James had come to the conclusion that the European working-class movement could not win without the African masses (nor the latter without the former), and that only the African masses—workers, peasants, and perhaps some farsighted intellectuals—fighting on their own terms could destroy imperialism. It was precisely this understanding that produced *The Black Jacobins* and *A History of Negro Revolt,* both published in 1938. These books were not written to appeal to white workers or a sympathetic liberal bourgeoisie. Rather, as Cedric Robinson so aptly put it, they were declarations of war.

IV

A History of Negro Revolt first appeared in September of 1938, just one month before James sailed for the United States. Commissioned by Raymond Postgate, a comrade of his in the

---

21 See Esedebe, *Pan-Africanism,* 123–25; Buhle, *C.L.R. James,* 55–56; J. Ayodele Langley, *Pan-Africanism and Nationalism in West Africa 1900–1945: A Study in Ideology and Social Classes* (London: Oxford University Press, 1973), 338.

22. Quoted in Robinson, *Black Marxism,* 383; for the whole review, see C.L.R. James, "'Civilizing' the 'Blacks': Why Britain Needs to Maintain her African Possessions," *New Leader,* May 29, 1936.

Independent Labour Party, the ninety-seven-page monograph was part of the *FACT* series published by the Party. This is what James had to say about it:

> Such a book had never been done before. I gathered a lot of material in it, and really I'm astonished now at how much there was that I didn't know. But the book has the virtue that there were all sorts of problems—like the struggles of women, market women in Africa and so on—that went into it, aside from the historical things like the Haitian revolution and the blacks in the American Civil War. . . . The book has a peculiar history. Postgate's name got the book sold in book-stores all over the country. When they found out what was in it some of them carefully hid it. There were places we went to where we found they had hidden it—they put it under a lot of other books, but when you asked for it they would say, yes, we have it.[23]

The book was hidden for good reason. Like the *Negro Worker,* the ITUC-NW organ which Padmore edited in the early 1930s, it was profoundly subversive.[24] It was a stinging indictment of colonialism, and James took no prisoners—not even his beloved France. Attacking France was not an easy thing to do, especially with fascism on the rise in Europe. The French not only let black colonials become deputies, governors, and cabinet ministers, but at the time James was writing.

---

23. C.L.R. James, *The Future in the Present: Selected Writings* (Westport, CN: Lawrence Hill and Co., 1977), 70.

24. The *Negro Worker* was also hidden; indeed, in Africa it was distributed in disguise. According to Robin Cohen, "some of the issues appeared in a cover bearing a cross and the title. *The Missionaries' Voice, The Path of the Cross, Organ of the African Methodist Episcopate of the London Missionary Society.* The second page carried the inscription 'Hearken ye that are oppressed and afflicted by manifold tribulations,' while the puzzled reader had to wait for the third page to read the more familiar slogan 'Proletarians of all Countries, Unite.'" Cohen, "Introduction" to *Forced Labour in Colonial Africa*, 14.

Prime Minister Leon Blum had become a sort of hero on the left. As the Socialist head of the French Popular Front government, Blum actively sought to neutralize fascist attempts to overthrow the Spanish Republic.[25] In the long run, none of this mattered to James. As he put it, "imperialism remains imperialism. . . . [T]he French have as black a record in Africa as any other imperialist nation" (68). And he proceeded to document that record and the efforts to resist. Just as he had tried to do as editor of *International African Opinion,* James wanted to make sure that colonialism would not be subordinated to the struggle against fascism, which is why he makes a point of saying that Africans under Italian fascism were no worse off than "an African in the Congo under democratic Belgium, or a Rhodesian copper miner" (69). The point is clear; there is no kinder, gentler colonialism.

What made this book even more subversive is the fact that James places black people at the center of world events; he characterizes uprisings of savages and religious fanatics as revolutionary movements; and he insists that the great Western revolutionaries of the modern world needed the Africans as much as the Africans needed them. The latter point is central to the entire book and is made forcefully in the first chapter on the Haitian Revolution—the world's only successful slave revolt, according to James. "Without the French Revolution," he asserts, "its success would have been impossible" (38). He is not simply talking about strategic support from Revolutionary France, especially since the nature of the alliance between the metropole and San Domingo's black rebels shifted with each regime. Rather, the ideals of liberty, equality, and fraternity transformed segments of the rank-and-file and the leadership, notably Toussaint L'Ouverture: "They embraced the revolutionary doctrine, they thought in republican terms. The result

---

25. Pierre Broue and Emile Temime, *The Revolution and the Civil War in Spain,* trans. Tony White (Cambridge: MIT Press, 1972), 321–65; David Carlton, "Eden, Blum, and the Origins of Non-intervention," *Journal of Contemporary History* 6 (January 1971): 40–55; M.D. Gallagher, "Leon Blum and the Spanish Civil War," *Journal of Contemporary History* 6 (January 1971): 56–64.

was that these slaves, lacking education, half-savage, and degraded in their slavery as only centuries of slavery can degrade, achieved a liberality in social aspiration and an elevation of political thought equivalent to anything similar that took place in France" (47). Yet, while a burning desire for liberty, articulated in the aims of the French Revolution, drove the slave, production relations on the plantation organized him. Here he echoes his classic line from *The Black Jacobins*. By "working and living together in gangs of hundreds on the huge sugar-factories which covered the North Plain, they were closer to a modern proletariat than any group of workers in existence at that time, and the rising was, therefore, a thoroughly prepared and organized mass movement" (40).[26]

But no matter how "proletarianized" the slaves were, they could not do it alone. In his discussion of the United States, James shows how a rich history of slave uprisings (in his words, they "revolted continuously") resulted in little more than heroic martyrs and a more repressive atmosphere. Victory was possi-

---

26. Where he ends this first chapter is significant. He does not take San Domingo into nationhood or deal with Toussaint's imprisonment under Napoleon. All we know is that the revolution in France retreated and "the old slave-owners regained influence and harassed the exhausted blacks"(50). By emphasizing the interdependency of Haiti and France, James missed an opportunity to illustrate a more important lesson: the need for complete and total independence from the colonizing country. Why this point is so clear in *The Black Jacobins* and missing from the first chapter of *A History of Negro Revolt* is a mystery. Perhaps the greatest mystery, however, is James's absolute silence on Haiti after 1800. The absence of modern Haiti is all the more surprising given the obvious influence Padmore's *Life and Struggles* had on the writing of this monograph. Padmore, for example, includes a fairly detailed discussion of Haitian opposition to American imperialism in 1929, of striking dockworkers shouting "DOWN WITH AMERICAN IMPERIALISM" while peasants marched from the countryside to the city. A movement of workers and peasants together, confronting a well-armed contingent of American marines, would have worked wonderfully in *A History of Negro Revolt*. After all, speaking of Africa James writes: "What the authorities fear most is a combination of the workers in the towns and the peasants in the interior." Padmore, *Life and Struggles*, 104; James, *A History of Pan-African Revolt*, 79.

ble, however, when the conditions resembled that of Haiti: during the Revolutionary Era when poor whites joined slaves, free
blacks and Mulattoes under the banner of liberty. But because
the United States was not a small Caribbean island, the slaves
and free blacks were always outnumbered and dispersed. More
significantly, slavery was much too important to capitalist development to abolish it on principle. Here we see possibly the be-
ginnings of James's influence on young Eric Williams, a former
student of his back in Trinidad. Anticipating Williams's classic study, *Slavery and Capitalism* (1944), James writes: "Slavery
made cotton king; cotton became the very life food of British
industries, it built up New England factories." Furthermore, the
growing impulse toward abolition was "not that sudden change
in the conscience of mankind so beloved of romantic and reactionary historians, but the climax of a gradual transformation
of world economy" (58).

The U.S. Civil War was the moment of truth, the world event
that gave these enslaved and half-starved black folk a chance.
James's analysis of the slaves' actions during the conflict is taken
straight from W.E.B. DuBois's monumental *Black Reconstruction
in America,* from his invocation of the "general strike" to his de-
scription of the slaves' hesitant responses toward the Union soldiers (60). Land was key. Indeed, it was the struggle for land that
rendered this newly created "peasantry" a revolutionary force,
for who understands better than the uprooted that land reform
was a necessary first step toward emancipation. "It was so in
France in 1789 and in Russia in 1917," James argues. "Peasants
today are politically alert as never before" (60). It was yet another challenge to Western Marxism—a tradition that had consistently distrusted the peasantry and invested all of its faith in
the proletariat.

Insisting that the peasantry—in this case ex-slaves—could
be a revolutionary force in and of itself was not entirely new.
Indian Communist M.N. Roy had made a similar point in his
1920 debate with Lenin over the national-colonial question.[27]

27. See Manabendra Nath Roy, *M.N Roy's Memoirs* (Bombay and
New York: Allied Publishers, 1964), 378; John Haithcox, *Communism
and Nationalism in India: M.N. Roy and Comintern Policy, 1920–1939*

What is unique is James's claim that revolutionary mass movements take forms that are often cultural and religious rather
than explicitly political. He forces the reader to re-examine these
seemingly odd movements with new eyes, to take the beliefs
and superstitions of Africans and African descendants seriously.
Perhaps he came to this conclusion independently, for his first
and only novel, *Minty Alley,* and his 1936 play about Toussaint
L'Ouverture, demonstrate an amazing sensitivity to the power of
religion and culture as major social and political forces in black
life.[28] Or perhaps he was moved, as many people were, when he
reached page 124 of DuBois's *Black Reconstruction* and found
his brilliant defense of the power of the Divine: "Foolish talk, all
of this, you say, of course; and that is because no American now
believes in his religion. Its facts are mere symbolism; its revela-
tion vague generalities; its ethics a matter of carefully balanced
gain. But to most of the four million black folk emancipated by
civil war, God was real. They knew Him. They had met Him personally in many a wild orgy of religious frenzy, or in the black
stillness of the night."[29]

Whatever the source, *A History of Negro Revolt* reveals James's
incredible faith in the masses and the supernatural forces that
moved them. The Watch Tower movement, for example, a millenarian movement that believed all Western governments were
evil and had to be replaced by a more just order, is described
here as one of the most powerful revolutionary forces in Africa
during the 1930s. Whereas most Marxist interpreters thought
such notions absurd and tended to dismiss religion as a diversion from the real struggle, James insisted that the ideas behind

---

(Princeton: Princeton University Press, 1971), 14–15; D.C. Grover,
M.N. Roy: A Study of Revolution and Reason in Indian Politics (Calcutta:
Minerva Associates, 1973), 2–13; V.B. Karnik, *M.N. Roy: A Political
Biography* (Bombay: Nav Jagriti Samaj, 1978), 107–10. Also, see note 10.

28. Drafts of *Minty Alley* (London: Seeker & Warburg, 1936) were
written years before the book was actually published, and "Toussaint
L'Ouverture" was produced in London in March of 1936.

29. W.E.B. DuBois, *Black Reconstruction in America: An Essay Toward a
History of the Part Which Black Folk Played in the Attempt to Reconstruct
Democracy in America, 1860–1880* (New York: Harcourt, Brace, 1935), 124.

the Watch Tower movement "represent political realities and
express political aspirations far more closely than programs and
policies of parties with millions of members, numerous journals and half a century of history behind them" (105). He also
discusses religious uprisings in Eastern and Central Africa—
most notably those led by John Chilembwe in Nyasaland and
Simon Kimbangu's cult in the Belgian Congo. If Marxists
thought these black Christian radicals were insignificant or less
important than, say, striking miners, the colonial state certainly
did not: even the smallest challenge from these "sects" was met
with immense repression and violence. At the very least, James
anticipated a later generation of historians who viewed these
religious-based movements as the source for some of the most
violent anti-colonial contests of the twentieth century.[30]

James's biggest "leap of faith" is his discussion of Garveyism.
By taking Marcus Garvey and his followers seriously, James di-
verged sharply from Padmore and most of his comrades in the
IASB. In fact, Padmore (who, along with other IASB activists,
used to heckle Garvey when he spoke at Hyde Park) had once
written that Garveyism was "the most reactionary expression
[of] Negro bourgeois nationalism" and therefore completely
"alien to the interests of the Negro toilers.[31] Although James
criticizes Garvey for his limited racial outlook, his collaboration with imperialists and American racists (notably the Ku
Klux Klan), and his inability to see the virtues of industrial organization, he nonetheless acknowledges that Garvey had built
the largest black mass movement in history. So rather than dis-

---

30. See, for example, Michael Adas, *Prophets of Rebellion: Millenarian
Protest Movements Against the European Colonial Order* (Chapel Hill:
University of North Carolina Press, 1979); Karen Fields, *Revival and
Rebellion in Colonial Africa* (Princeton: Princeton University Press,
1985); Robin D.G. Kelley, "The Religious Odyssey of African Radicals:
Notes on the Communist Party of South Africa, 1921–1934," *Radical
History Review* 51 (1991): 5–24; Vittorio Lanternari, *The Religions of the
Oppressed: A Study of Modern Messianic Cults* (New York: Knopf, 1963);
George Shepperson and Thomas Price, *Independent African: John
Chilembwe and the Origins, Settings and Significance of the Nyasaland
Native Rising of 1915* (Edinburgh: Edinburgh University Press, 1958).

31. Padmore, *Life and Struggles*, 126.

miss Garvey as a charlatan, James tries to understand his appeal. He had no other choice; throughout *A History of Negro Revolt* James hammers home the point that the masses have the capacity to move on their own, to throw up their own leaders, to understand the situation at hand. If Garvey had merely duped his followers, then a good proportion of the black world were dupes.

The success of Garveyism, James suggests, has a lot to do with the peculiar and complex nature of racism. While many of his radical contemporaries focused in on the political, economic, and structural aspects of racism, James's chapter on Garvey explores its cultural and psychological dimensions. Instead of emphasizing how racism is used to divide the working class, he concentrates on how it is lived and experienced, "how the Negro is made to feel his color at every turn" (88). In a world where the very humanity of dark-skinned people was perpetually assaulted and questioned, Garvey gave his followers a sense of history and personhood. By linking the entire black world to Africa and to each other, he turned a national minority into an international majority. In James's words, "He made the American Negro conscious of his African origin and created for the first time a feeling of international solidarity among Africans and people of African descent" (94).[32]

James's recognition of the revolutionary potential of black nationalism should have made *A History of Negro Revolt* an instant classic among the Left. By the late 1930s, virtually all left-wing movements were floundering on the "Negro Question," including the Communists who had abandoned self-determination in favor of the Popular Front. In 1939, a year after James left England for the United States, he tried to persuade Leon Trotsky himself at a summit meeting in Coyoacan, Mexico, that the Left needs to support autonomous black movements on their own terms, and that the struggle against racism and for democratic rights is primary to the struggle for socialism. Black nationalism, he insisted,

---

32. Paul Buhle makes this point in *C.L.R. James: The Artist as Revolutionary*, 57.

was not some diversion from the class struggle but a revolutionary force to be reckoned with.[33]

Unfortunately, James was about three decades too early, or the Left was three decades too late. In the meantime, *A History of Negro Revolt* remained hidden just as James remembered. And to the many Marxists who still believed that the proletarian revolution would take the form of an industrial workers' uprising with themselves in the vanguard, the book made no sense. It was not until a new generation of Afro-coifed young militants discovered this little book that its full import would be recognized.

V

When Drum and Spear Press, a black nationalist–oriented publishing house in Washington, D.C., decided to inaugurate their company by re-issuing *A History of Negro Revolt* in 1969, James had just been allowed to re-enter the United States the year before (he had been deported to England in 1953).[34] The Press was an outgrowth of the Drum and Spear Bookstore, a black activist–oriented outlet founded in 1967 by about a half dozen former Southern Civil Rights organizers who had moved back to Washington. In addition to running the bookstore, they established a community school called the Center for Black Education. Frustrated by the dearth of books by or about black people, the Drum and Spear collective decided to publish their own books and bring important works back into print.[35]

---

33. For transcripts of the debate between James ("J.R. Johnson") and Trotsky, see *Leon Trotsky on Black Nationalism and Self-Determination* (New York: Pathfinder Press, 1978).

34. Haskell House Publishers in New York also published *A History of Negro Revolt* in its original form in 1969, apparently without James's consent or his knowledge.

35. Author phone interview with Charlie Cobb, August 31, 1994. (Cobb was a founding member of Drum and Spear Bookstore and the press.) Beyond James's book, the only other title they published was a children's book written and illustrated by Jennifer Lawson titled *Children of Africa.*

By this time, members of the collective had grown fairly close to C.L.R., who had moved to Washington a year after Drum and Spear Bookstore was founded. They had come to know James through Federal City College, some of them having been fellow faculty members there. His 16th Street apartment soon became a kind of meeting ground for these young activist/intellectuals to discuss black liberation, community organizing, history, sociology, politics, and a whole host of issues. Indeed, James not only participated in discussions leading to the founding of Drum and Spear Press, but it was he who volunteered *A History of Negro Revolt* as its first title. The Drum and Spear collective was happy to oblige, for they clearly respected James as an elder mentor for their generation. In the introduction to the new edition, Marvin Holloway of the Center for Black Education characterized James as a living revolutionary who had seen and experienced struggles that most young militants only read about. At a time "when black people throughout the world are clamoring for self-knowledge," the sixty-eight-year-old C.L.R. "has become a great source of wisdom and counsel to youth in the Resistance Movement" (vii and viii). And what better time to be a source of wisdom and counsel? The year he returned to the United States, Martin Luther King, Jr., had been assassinated, the ghettos were in flames, the Black Panther Party was making front-page news, militant college students were demonstrating for Black Studies Departments, and Republican Richard Nixon was elected president on the promise of crushing the wave of dissent that threatened to destroy American civilization. James himself had just concluded a lecture tour in East and West Africa, so he was returning with first-hand knowledge of the situation in the newly independent African states.

Along with the new title, *A History of Pan-African Revolt*, James added a forty-three-page Epilogue titled "The History

By about 1973 the store and the press literally faded out of existence, in part due to the effect the riots had on black businesses on 14th St., and in part due to the usual difficulties that arise with activist-oriented enterprises. Their business decisions were driven by political motives rather than profit motives.

of Pan-African Revolt: A Summary 1939–1969," which briefly explores decolonization in Africa, the Civil Rights movement in the United States, and recent conflicts in the Caribbean. The Epilogue is important, for it reflects James's intellectual and political development since the book first appeared three decades earlier as a FACT *monograph of the British Independent Labour Party. He does not simply attach more episodes of black rebellion to the story; he adds substantively to the conceptual framework he had developed in the first edition.*

First, the Epilogue gives us an even stronger defense of black nationalism than the earlier chapters had. Of course, by the 1960s black nationalism itself had become more forceful and radical, adopting a rhetoric and style far more militant than anything Marcus Garvey had imagined. Some black nationalists in the United States talked of armed struggle, expressed solidarity with other anti-colonial movements, learned African languages, and, most importantly, identified with the ghetto poor. But James's growing appreciation for the revolutionary potential of black nationalism can be traced back much further—at least to the Second World War. As a member of the Socialist Workers Party and regular contributor to its newspaper, the *Militant,* James was deeply impressed with the rise of black self-organization and activism during the war.[36] African American trade union membership rose from 150,000 in 1935 to 1.2 million by 1945; civil rights organizations recruited tens of thousands of new members (the NAACP, for example, had grown ten-fold during the war); and mainstream black leaders insisted on a "double victory" against racism at home and fascism abroad.[37] The Double-V campaign, embodied power-

---

36. Some of James's articles for the *Militant* are reprinted in C.L.R. James, et al., *Fighting Racism in World War II* (New York: Monad Press, 1980). James's understanding of the impact of World War II on African-Americans is also made abundantly clear in his recently published 1950 manuscript, *American Civilization,* eds. Anna Grimshaw and Keith Hart, (London: Basil Blackwell, 1993), 200–11.

37. Manning Marable, *Race, Reform, and Rebellion: The Second Reconstruction in Black America, 1945–1982* (Jackson, MS: University Press of Mississippi, 1984), 13–14; Herbert Garfinkel, *When Negroes*

fully in A. Philip Randolph's threatened march on Washington in 1943, partly articulated the sense of hope and anger that a lot of black people shared. As black journalist Roi Ottley observed during the early years of the war, one could not walk the streets of Harlem and not notice a profound change. "Listen to the way Negroes are talking these days! . . . [B]lack men have become noisy, aggressive, and sometimes defiant."[38]

By the war's end, James was convinced of the necessity of black nationalism as an essential element of the black freedom struggle. As early as 1945, he believed that "the Negro is nationalist to his heart and is perfectly right to be so. His racism, his nationalism, are a necessary means of giving him strength, self-respect and organization *in order to fight for integration into American society.*" Two years later, in an important document titled "The Revolutionary Answer to the Negro Problem in the U.S.A," he echoed these sentiments and pushed even further. By virtue of their experiences in the United States under racism and capitalism, he argued, black people were inherently revolutionary. "Anyone who knows them," he concluded, "who knows their history, is able to talk to them intimately, watches them in their own theatres, watches them at their dances, watches them in their churches, reads their press with a discerning eye, must recognize that although their social force may not be able to compare with the social force of a corresponding number of or-

---

March: The March on Washington Movement in the Organizational Politics of the FEPC (Glencoe, Ill.: The Free Press, 1959).

38. Roi Ottley, *New World A-Comin': Inside Black America* (Boston: Houghton Mifflin, 1943), 306. On black militancy during the war, see Richard Dalfiume, "The 'Forgotten Years' of the Negro Revolution," *Journal of American History* 55 (June 1968): 90–106; Herbert Garfinkel, *When Negroes March;* Peter J. Kellogg, "Civil Rights Consciousness in the 1940s," *The Historian* 42 (November 1979): 18–41; Harvard Sitkoff, *A New Deal for Blacks: The Emergence of Civil Rights as a National Issue* (Oxford and New York: Oxford University Press, 1978), 298–325; Robert Korstad and Nelson Lichtenstein, "Opportunities Found and Lost: Labor, Radicals, and the Early Civil Rights Movement," *Journal of American History* 75 (December 1988): 786–811; Herbert Shapiro, *White Violence and Black Response: From Reconstruction to Montgomery* (Amherst: University of Massachusetts Press, 1988), 301–48.

ganized workers, the hatred of bourgeois society and the readiness to destroy it when the opportunity should present itself, rests among them to a degree greater than in any other section of the population in the United States."[39]

Thus the rise of Black Power did not surprise James at all. What surprised his old left-wing supporters, however, was how little he spoke about the proletariat during this period. Although he defensively reminded his critics that he was "still a man of the proletariat," the Epilogue, like many of his speeches in the late 1960s, says less about working class struggles than the previous chapters. Instead, the dominant forces in the post-1938 black revolution are students, Civil Rights activists, intellectuals. This shift in emphasis is a product of the time and the context. James was quite taken with the Black Power movement, especially the more left-leaning spokespersons like Stokely Carmichael and H. Rap Brown. In a 1967 speech, for example, he dismissed charges that Carmichael was a racialist and suggested that his vision was much closer to socialism than the white Left realized. Citing Lenin to prove his point, he argued vehemently that the Black Power movement constitutes a challenge to capital and therefore should be backed by the Left. Moreover, he reminded his audience of the importance of supporting black self-organization, irrespective of contradictions the movement might exhibit: "Who are we to say 'Yes, you are entitled to say this but not to say that; you are entitled to do this but not to do that'? If we know the realities of Negro oppression in the U.S.A. (and if you don't we should keep our mouths shut until we do), then we should guide ourselves by a West Indian expression which I recommend to you: *what he do, he well do.* Let me repeat that: what the American Negroes do is, as far as we are concerned, well done. They will take their chances, they will risk their liberty, they will risk their lives if need be. *The decisions are theirs.*"[40]

---

39. Letter to Constance Webb (1945) in *The C.L.R. James Reader*, 146; "The Revolutionary Answer to the Negro Problem in the U.S.A.," in *The C.L.R. James Reader*, 188–89; Paul Buhle, "Marxism in the U.S.A.," in *C.L.R. James: His Life and Work*, 32; also see Buhle, *C.L.R. James: The Artist as Revolutionary*, 70–73.

40. "Black Power," in *The C.L.R. James Reader*, 369.

. Where Black Power counted most, however, was in Africa. Clearly the linchpin of the Pan-African revolt was the continent itself, and the struggle that had the greatest impact on James took place in the Gold Coast—the British West African colony that became modern Ghana in 1957. The Gold Coast revolution and its esteemed leader, Kwame Nkrumah, is the centerpiece of the Epilogue. He believed, as did many of his peers, that Ghana would be the beacon lighting the way toward the emancipation of black Africa.[41]

James had met Nkrumah years before while he was a student at Lincoln University, a historically black institution in Pennsylvania. With Padmore practically training Nkrumah to lead the independence struggle in his homeland, James had a tremendous amount of confidence in this young man. But it was his visit to Ghana in 1957 that really opened his eyes to the political importance of this small West African country. So moved by the events he witnessed in Accra, James quickly postponed plans for a pamphlet on Hungary and immediately set out to write a small book on Ghana. The level of militancy and self-organization he observed challenged earlier theories of revolution, including some of the ideas put forth in his own *Black Jacobins*. Now he questioned the extent to which revolutions in Western Europe and African revolutions were interdependent. While James worried that Ghana, like other newly independent nations, had the potential of being overtaken by bureaucratic corruption, he was nonetheless convinced that something different was happening under Nkrumah: true grassroots democracy. By making Ghana the center of a continent-wide African liberation movement, James surmised, Nkrumah would keep the revolution permanent. And by moving immediately to socialism through state intervention and "initiating new so-

---

41. During the 1950s, both Padmore and Richard Wright had written books on Ghana, and James would follow with his own in 1977. George Padmore, *The Gold Coast Revolution: The Struggle of an African People from Slavery to Freedom* (London: D. Dobson, 1953); Richard Wright, *Black Power: A Record of Reactions in the Land of Pathos* (New York: Harper & Brothers, 1954); C.L.R. James, *Nkrumah and the Ghana Revolution* (Westport, CT.: Lawrence and Hill, Co., 1977).

cial relations from below," Ghana could make the revolutionary transition that neither the USSR nor Eastern Europe was
capable of making.[42]

By the mid-1960s, however, his enthusiasm for Nkrumah
and Ghana had diminished. He admitted that the new society
he had hoped for was not built, and that Nkrumah allowed
bureaucratic corruption to take over. Ghana's failure provided
James with two critical lessons for constructing postcolonial society, both of which carried over into *A History of Pan-African
Revolt*. First, a revolutionary society cannot be created unless
the colonial state is completely dismantled. Second, the new
generation of African leaders needs to create and sustain democratic institutions throughout the country. Even if those institutions are critical of the government, a new society cannot be
built without them. These two points bear the obvious imprint
of Frantz Fanon, whose book *The Wretched of the Earth* James
had read before writing the Epilogue (107). While James understood the importance of dismantling the colonial state in
theory, he knew in practice that the African leaders of the newly
independent nations tended to be Western-educated civil servants who were products of the colonial state and thus had a
personal stake in maintaining it.[43]

What was needed to rid Africa of its bureaucratic petite
bourgeoisie was uncompromising revolt, permanent revolution
from below. The political and cultural resources for such a revolution, he argues, can be found in traditional African society.
Once again, James displays his enormous faith in the forms of
organization and culture created by the masses themselves. But

---

42. Letter of March 20, 1957, in Grimshaw, ed.. *The C.L.R. James Reader*,
269–70; see also, James, *Nkrumah*, 50–158 *passim*.; Manning Marable,
"The Fall of Kwame Nkrumah," in Buhle, ed., *C.L.R. James: His Life and
Work*, 39–47. James was so taken by Ghana, that in his March 20, 1957,
letter (cited above) he actually suggested that young blacks from the
West emigrate there! Recall that in these very pages he calls Garvey's
emigration scheme "pitiable rubbish" (92).

43. "The Rise and Fall of Nkrumah," in *The C.L.R. James Reader*, 354–
61; C.L.R. James, "Kwame Nkrumah of Ghana," in *At the Rendezvous of
Victory*, 180.

unlike the earlier chapters, the Epilogue looks to these forms not just as sources of resistance to imperialism but as the basis for a new society. "There are also the democratic instincts and practices of the African tribes," he observed in 1957, "not those damned chiefs with their feathers and umbrellas and stools, made into petty tyrants by the British Government, but the old tribal method of appointing them by election and throwing them out if they were unsatisfactory."[44] Here he makes his sharpest break yet from the European Marxist tradition. Socialism, he concluded, need not be built on the logic of modern industrial organization; it can be built on pre-capitalist traditions of democracy and communal social relations.

James obviously came to this conclusion independently, but so did several African nationalists, including Senegal's Leopold Senghor and Tanzania's Julius Nyerere.[45] When Ghana failed to live up to its promises, James decided that Tanzania was now Africa's hope for the future. Indeed, he ends this book as well as his study of Nkrumah with a paean to Nyerere's approach to socialist transformation titled "Always Out of Africa." In hindsight, of course, we know that Nyerere's attempt to establish a collectively-run national economy based on communal villages was an utter disaster, that his regime repressed strikes and opposition movements, and that his party—the Tanzanian African National Union (TANU)—had more than its share of

---

44. Letter of March 20, 1957, in *The C.L.R. James Reader*, 270.

45. See Leopold Senghor, *Nation et Voie Africaine du Socialisme* (Paris: Editions Presence Africaine, 1961); Julius K. Nyerere, *Freedom and Socialism* (New York: Oxford University Press, 1968); Julius K. Nyerere, "African Socialism: Ujamaa in Practice," in *Pan-Africanism*, eds. Robert Chrisman and Nathan Hare (Indianapolis and New York: The Bobbs-Merrill Co., 1974), 107–13. That James was enthusiastic about Nyerere and had nothing to say about Senghor is telling. While Senghor engaged the great philosophers—Hegel, Marx, Engels, and Lenin—and developed a very sophisticated argument for the synthesis of modern socialism and traditional culture, he had not done much in the way of implementation. Talk and no action never impressed James. Perhaps he was thinking of Senghor, among others, when he dismissed most efforts at building "African socialism" as "bureaucratic balderdash" (132).

corruption.[46] But when James wrote the Epilogue, TANU's famous "Arusha Declaration" laying out the philosophy and structure of Tanzania's African socialist society was less than two years old. And, on paper, it was an incredibly progressive document. With bylaws requiring party and government leaders to be "either a Peasant or a Worker, and should in no way be associated with the practices of Capitalism or Feudalism," (128) how could any socialist *not* be impressed? What attracted James more than anything was Nyerere's ideas for public education. Nyerere planned to establish schools that would prepare students to create a socialist society based on traditional culture. James believed these were the key grassroots institutions that could sustain democracy and ultimately destroy the colonial state.[47]

The book closes on a hopeful note. Nyerere had not only found a revolutionary path for Africa but made the most important contribution to Marxist thought since Lenin. As we now know, James was wrong on the first count, and depending on who you talk to, some might say he was wrong on both counts. The idea that Africans ought to draw on their own resources and cultures in order to build a socialist society is hard to contest; the problem lies in the belief that pre-colonial African societies were inherently democratic and practiced a form of "primitive communism" that could lay the groundwork for modern socialism. Several historians have challenged this romantic view of Africa's past, exposing the level of class and gender exploitation internal to so-called "traditional" societies.[48] That James ac-

---

46. Three excellent critiques of "Ujamaa" and Nyerere's romantic notion of African Communalism are Issa Shivji, *Class Struggles in Tanzania* (New York: Monthly Review Press, 1976); A.M. Babu, *African Socialism or Socialist Africa?* (London: Zed Press, 1981); Arnold Temu and Bonaventure Swai, *Historians and Africanist History: A Critique* (London: Zed Press, 1983).

47. In addition to the Epilogue, see Buhle, *C.L.R. James: The Artist as Revolutionary*, 140–41.

48. A similar critique of James is made by South African Trotskyist Baruch Hirson, who is also a historian of the South African Left. See his "Communalism and Socialism in Africa: The Misdirection of C.L.R.

cepted this view does not diminish in any way James's brilliance or the profound insights this book has to offer. Rather, it simply means that he is no fortune teller. Yet, what I find quite puzzling is his complete silence on Tanzania throughout the remainder of his life. Even after sharp criticisms of the TANU government were leveled by radical intellectuals within Tanzania, James apparently never responded or corrected his earlier assessments—at least not in print. Indeed, he included his unaltered assessment of Nyerere in *Nkrumah and the Ghana Revolution* which appeared in 1977, one year after Issa Shivji, a Tanzanian Marxist historian, thoroughly excised the utter bankruptcy of Nyerere's policies in his highly acclaimed book, *Class Struggles in Tanzania*. After *Nkrumah and the Ghana Revolution* was published, however, the seventy-six-year-old radical could no longer maintain the herculean pace that made him one of the most prolific scholar/activists in the Western world. His relative silence on Africa, as with many other issues, should not come as a surprise.[49]

VI

A History of Pan-African Revolt is one of those rare books that continues to strike a chord of urgency, even half a century

---

James," *Searchlight South Africa* 4 (February 1990): 64–73.

49. Nevertheless, the fact that James says nothing about Portugal's African colonies (Mozambique, Angola, Guinea-Bissau, and the Cape Verde Islands) in the Epilogue and only occasionally discussed them in the 1970s and 1980s was somewhat surprising. The anti-colonial movements there not only took up arms against the Portuguese and adopted Marxism-Leninism in some form or another, but they created liberated zones where revolutionaries and villagers attempted to build socialist-oriented communities in the midst of war. See, for example, Basil Davidson, *In the Eye of the Storm: Angola's People* (Garden City, NY: Anchor Books, 1973); Thomas Henriksen, "People's War in Angola, Mozambique and Guinea-Bissau," *The Journal of Modern African Studies* 14, no. 3 (1976): 377–99; Amilcar Cabral, *Revolution in Guinea* (New York: Monthly Review Press, 1969); Jack McCulloch, *In the Twilight of Revolution: The Political Theory of Amilcar Cabral* (London: Zed Books, 1983).

after it was first published. Time and time again, its lessons have proven to be valuable and relevant for understanding liberation movements in Africa and the diaspora. Each generation who has had the opportunity to read this small book finds new insights, new lessons, new visions for their own age. When the *"Race Today* Collective," a gathering of people of color in London who edited the progressive multicultural magazine of the same title, decided to bring back into print *A History of Negro Revolt* in 1985, they found the book as meaningful to their world as it was to the African and Caribbean radicals who had walked the same streets fifty years earlier. Although Ethiopia was not the pressing issue this time around, many of the battles they fought would have been familiar to the 1930s generation: South Africa, Grenada, the riots in Brixton, racist violence against immigrants, the struggle for black political empowerment:

> We publish this third edition at a moment when the course of negro [*sic*] revolt enters a period of increased acceleration. The masses of Caribbean Peoples are in open revolt against American imperialism. Such is the intensity of the movement that it takes the might of the American military to contain it. South Africa is stirring and the end of the apartheid regime cannot be long delayed. The emergence of Jesse Jackson, as a major figure in American politics, can only be explained by the mass movement from below of American blacks.
>
> We are certain that *A History of Negro Revolt* contributes to an understanding of these events and will inform action in a way in which few historical documents have.[50]

In reading and re-reading this classic text, we ought to reflect on our own times and determine how this book might inform our own actions. What can this book tell us about post-apartheid South Africa under president Nelson Mandela? The desperate situation in James's beloved Haiti? "Ethnic cleansing"

---

50. *A History of Negro Revolt* (London: Race Today Publications, 1985), 5. Why the *Race Today* Collective chose to revert back to the term "negro" is unclear.

in Rwanda? What of heightened racism and anti-Semitism in Europe and the United States? The incredibly high rates of unemployment and violence in Western capitalist cities and the Left's virtual abandonment of America's black ghettos?

No piece of literature can substitute for a crystal ball, and only religious fundamentalists believe that a book can provide comprehensive answers to all questions. But if nothing else, *A History of Pan-African Revolt* leaves us with two incontrovertible facts. First, as long as black people are denied freedom, humanity, and a decent standard of living, they will continue to revolt. Second, unless these revolts involve the ordinary masses and take place on their own terms, they have no hope of succeeding. As James once said of the revolution in Ghana, their struggles may appear "sometimes pathetic, sometimes vastly comic, ranging from the sublime to the ridiculous, but always vibrant with the life that only a mass of ordinary people can give."[51] And if world events are on their side, they just might win.

Robin D.G. Kelley, Haitian Independence Day, 1994

---

51. C.L.R. James, "Colonialism and National Liberation in Africa: The Gold Coast Revolution," in *National Liberation: Revolution in the Third World*, eds. Norman Miller and Roderick Aya (New York: The Free Press, 1971), 136.

A History of Pan-African Revolt

San Domingo

1

The history of the Negro in his relation to European civilization falls into two divisions, the Negro in Africa and the Negro in America and the West Indies. Up to the 'eighties of the last century, only one-tenth of Africa was in the hands of Europeans. Until that time, therefore, it is the attempt of the Negro in the Western World to free himself from his burdens which has political significance in Western history. In the last quarter of the nineteenth century European civilization turned again to Africa, this time not for slaves to work the plantations of America but for actual control of territory and population. Today (1938) the position of Africans in Africa is one of the major problems of contemporary politics. An attempt is made here to give some account and analysis of Negro revolts through the centuries; in the days of slavery; in Africa during the last half-century; and in America and the West Indies today.

It is impossible in this space to deal with the slave-trade and slavery; the same consideration has made it necessary to omit accounts of the early revolts in the West Indies and the incessant guerrilla warfare carried on in all the islands by the maroons (or runaway slaves) against their former masters. Negroes have continually revolted and once in Dutch Guiana the revolting slaves held almost the entire colony for months. But in the eighteenth century the greatest colony in the West Indies was French San Domingo (now Haiti) and there took place the most famous of all Negro revolts. It forms a useful starting point.

1789 is a landmark in the history of Negro revolt in the West Indies. The only successful Negro revolt, the only successful slave revolt in history, had its roots in the French Revolution, and without the French Revolution its success would have been impossible.

During the eighteenth century French San Domingo developed a fabulous prosperity and by 1789 was taking 40,000 slaves a year. In 1789 the total foreign trade of Britain was twenty-seven million pounds, of which the colonial trade accounted for only five million pounds. The total foreign trade of France was seventeen million pounds, of which San Domingo alone was responsible for eleven millions. "Sad irony of human history," comments Jaures, "the fortunes created at Bordeaux, at Nantes, by the slave-trade gave to the bourgeoisie that pride which needed liberty and contributed to human emancipation." But the colonial system of the eighteenth century ordained that whatever manufactured goods the colonists needed could be bought only in France. They could sell their produce only to France. The goods were to be transported only in French ships. Colonial planters and the Home Government were thus in bitter and constant conflict, the very conflict which had resulted in the American War of Independence. The American colonists gained their freedom in 1783, and in less than five years the British attitude to the slave-trade changed.

Previous to 1783 they had been the most successful practitioners of the slave-trade in the world. But now not only was America

gone, but it was British ships which were supplying a large proportion of the 40,000 slaves a year which were the basis of San
Domingo's prosperity. The trade of San Domingo almost doubled
between 1783 and 1789. The British West Indian colonies were in
comparison poor, and with the loss of America, were of diminish-
ing importance. The monopoly of the West Indian sugar planters galled the rising industrial bourgeoisie, potential free-traders.
Adam Smith and Arthur Young, economists of the coming industrial age, condemned the expensiveness of slave labor. India offered
the example of a country where the laborer cost only a penny a
day, did not have to be bought, and did not brand his master as a
slave-owner. In 1787 the Abolitionist Society was formed and the
British Government, which only a few years before had threatened
to sack a Governor of Jamaica if he tampered with the slave-trade
in any shape or form, now changed its mind. If the slave-trade was
brought to a sudden close, San Domingo would be ruined. The
British islands would lose nothing, for they had as many slaves
as they seemed likely to need. The abolitionists it is true worked
very hard, and Clarkson, for instance, was a very honest and sincere man. Many people were moved by their propaganda. But that
a considerable and influential section of British men of business
thought that the slave-trade was not only a blot on the national
name but a growing hole in the national pocket, was the point that
mattered. The evidence for this is given in detail in the writer's
Black Jacobins published in 1938 with a revised edition in 1963.

The Abolition Society was formed in 1787. France at that
time was stirring with the revolution, and the French humanitar-
ians formed a parallel society, "The Friends of the Negro." They
preached the abolition not only of the slave-trade but of slavery
as well, and Brissot, Mirabeau, Condorcet, Robespierre, many
of the great names of the revolution, were among the members.
They ignored or minimized the fact that, unlike Britain, two-
thirds of France's overseas trade was bound up with the traffic.
Wilberforce and Clarkson encouraged them, gave the society
money, and did active propaganda in France. This was the position in Europe when the French Revolution began.

San Domingo possessed at that time 500,000 slaves, and only
30,000 Mulattoes and about the same number of whites. But the

slave-owners of San Domingo at once embraced the revolution, and as each section interpreted liberty, equality and fraternity to suit itself, civil war was soon raging between them. Some of the rich whites, especially those who owed debts to French merchants, wanted to follow the example of America and virtually rule themselves. The Mulattoes wanted to be rid of their disabilities, the poor whites wanted to become masters and officials like the rich whites. These classes fought fiercely with one another. The white colonists lynched and murdered Mulattoes for daring to claim equality. But the whites themselves were divided into royalists and revolutionaries. The French revolutionary legislatures first of all evaded the question of Mulatto rights, then gave some of the Mulattoes rights, then took the rights away again. Mulattoes and whites fought, and under the stress of necessity began to arm their slaves. The news from France, the slogans of liberty, equality and fraternity, the political excitement in San Domingo, the civil war between rich whites, poor whites and Mulattoes, it was these things which after two years awoke the sleeping slaves to revolution. By July, 1791, in the thickly populated North they were planning a rising.

The slaves worked on the land, and, like revolutionary peasants everywhere, they aimed at the extermination of their masters. But, working and living together in gangs of hundreds on the huge sugar-factories which covered the North Plain, they were closer to a modern proletariat than any group of workers in existence at that time, and the rising was, therefore, a thoroughly prepared and organized mass movement.

On a night in August a tropical storm raged, with lightning and gusts of wind and heavy showers of rain. Carrying torches to light their way, the leaders of the revolt met in an open space in the thick forests of the Morne Rouge, a mountain overlooking Cap François, the largest town. There Boukman, the leader, after Voodoo incantations and the sucking of the blood of a stuck pig, gave the last instructions.

That very night they began. Each slave-gang murdered its masters and burnt the plantation to the ground. The slaves destroyed tirelessly. They knew that as long as those plantations stood, their lot would be to labor on them until they dropped.

They violated all the women who fell into their hands, often on the bodies of their still bleeding husbands, fathers and brothers. But they did not maintain this vengeful spirit for long. As the revolution gained territory they spared many of the men, women and children whom they surprised on plantations. To prisoners of war alone they remained merciless. They tore out their flesh with red-hot pincers, they roasted them on slow fires, they sawed a carpenter between his boards. Yet on the whole, they never approached in their tortures the savageries to which they themselves had been subjected.

The white planters refused to take the slave revolt seriously. They continued to intrigue against the Mulattoes and to threaten the French Government. But as the chaos grew, the rich royalists swallowed their color prejudice and united with the Mulattoes against the revolutionary planters. Meanwhile the insurrection prospered, until a few weeks after it began there were about a hundred thousand revolting slaves divided into large bands. The leaders were Jean-Francois and Biassou, and Toussaint L'Ouverture joined them a month after the revolt began. He was forty-six, first his master's coachman and afterward, owing to his intelligence, placed in charge of the livestock on the estate, a post usually held by a white man. He had a smattering of education, but he could not write correct French, and usually spoke Creole i.e. the local French patois.

Baffled in their first spring at the city, these leaders did not know what to do, and when the French Government sent Commissioners who boasted of the armed forces (quite imaginary) which were on their way, the Negro leaders sought to betray their followers. They wrote to the Commissioners promising that in return for the freedom of a few hundred they would cooperate in leading the others back into slavery and would join in hunting down the recalcitrant. Toussaint, in charge of the negotiations, reduced the offer from 400 to 60. The French Commissioners gladly accepted, but the white planters with great scorn refused. Toussaint therefore gave up hopes of even a treacherous solution and began to train a small band of soldiers from among the hordes.

The French legislature was by this time under the leadership of Brissot and the Girondins. These managed to persuade the colonial interests that it was to their advantage to give all rights to the Mulattoes, and in April 1792, this became law. But Brissot, doughty propagandist for abolition before he came to power, now would not go a step further than rights for Mulattoes. Far from abolishing slavery, he and his government dispatched a force to crush the slave revolt. These troops landed in San Domingo, but before they could begin the attack, events had occurred in Paris which altered the whole course of the French Revolution, and with it, the black revolution in San Domingo.

On August 10, 1792, the Paris masses, tired of the equivocations and indecision of the Parliamentarians, stormed the Tuileries and dragged the Bourbons off the throne. A wave of enthusiasm for liberty swept over France and from indifference to slavery at the beginning of the revolution, revolutionary France now hated no section of the aristocracy so much as the colonial whites, "the aristocrats of the skin." In San Domingo the news of August 10 so split the slave-owners that the civil war between them which had ended began again. Every conflict among the slave-owners was a source of added strength to the slaves.

By February 1793 war had broken out between revolutionary France and England and Spain. The Spaniards in Spanish San Domingo from the start had helped the slaves against the French. Now they offered them a formal alliance and the slaves trooped over to join Spain. Whether France was a republic or reactionary monarchy, made no difference to the colonial slave if each was prepared to keep him in slavery. Toussaint L'Ouverture went with the others but he secretly offered to the French the services of his trained band if they would abolish slavery. They refused. He made a similar offer to the Spanish commander who likewise refused. Toussaint decided to stay where he was and watch developments. Sonthonax, the French Commissioner, at his wits' end, threatened by Britain and Spain and increasingly deserted by the French blacks, abolished slavery as his last chance of gaining some support. His maneuver failed. Toussaint remained with the Spaniards and won most of the North Province for them. For the planters, abolition was the last straw and they offered the colony to Pitt, who dispatched an expedition from Europe to capture the French colonies in the West Indies. The British carried all before

them, and by June 1794 over two-thirds of San Domingo and almost every French island of importance were in the hands of the
British. The rest seemed only a matter of days.

But meanwhile the revolution had been rising in France.
Before the end of 1793 Brissot had been swept out of power.
Robespierre and the Mountain ruled and led the revolution
against its enemies at home and abroad. By this time all revolutionary France had embraced the cause of the slaves, many refusing even to touch coffee as being drenched with the blood of their
own human kind. On February 4, 1794, the Convention abolished slavery without a debate. "The English are beaten," shouted
Danton. "Pitt and his plots are riddled." The great master of revolutionary tactics had seen far. The British fleet prevented assistance going to the hard pressed colored revolution but the decree
of abolition would throw the blacks wholeheartedly on the side
of the French. Toussaint joined the French at once, and slaugh-
tered his Spanish allies, white and black, of yesterday; while in
Martinique, Guadeloupe, and the other French colonies, the
black slaves, singing the *Ça Ira* and the *Marseillaise* and dressed
in the colors of the Republic, began to drive the British out of the
French islands, and then carried the war into British territory.

Spain made peace, in 1795, and by 1799 the British had been
driven out of San Domingo and most of the French colonies
by Negro slaves and Mulattoes. Fortescue, the Tory historian of
the British army, gives a vivid account of this colossal disaster.
Britain lost 100,000 men in the West Indies in these four years,
two and a half times as many as Wellington lost in the whole
of the Peninsular War. Fever took a heavy toll, but Toussaint
L'Ouverture, and Rigaud, a Mulatto, in San Domingo; and Victor
Hugues, a Mulatto, in Martinique and the smaller islands, won
one of the most important victories in the French revolutionary
wars. Aided by the fever, they, in Fortescue's phrase, "practically
destroyed the British army." For six years Britain was tied up in the
West Indies, and to quote Fortescue once more, if Britain played
so insignificant a part in the attack on revolutionary France in
Europe during the first six years of the war, the answer is to be
found in "the two fatal words, San Domingo." The part played by
the blacks in the success of the great French Revolution has never

received adequate recognition. The revolution in Europe will ne-
glect colored workers at its peril.

With the British driven out, L'Ouverture occupied a powerful position. He was Commander-in-Chief, appointed by the
French Government, of a French army, with white officers under him. But as soon as the British were driven out, the French
started to intrigue against him. They engineered a quarrel between himself and Rigaud, the Mulatto, whence was fought a bitter civil war. Toussaint was victorious, then brought Spanish San
Domingo under his control. He established a strong government
over the whole island, drew up a constitution which made him
First Consul for life, and gave San Domingo "dominion status";
concentrating all the power in his own hands, he governed. In
eighteen months he had restored a colony, devastated by years
of civil war, to two-thirds of its former prosperity. He was a des-
pot, confining his laborers to the plantations and brooking no
interference with his will under harsh penalties. But he protected
the laborers from the injustice of their former owners. He saw
that they were paid their wages. He established free trade and
religious toleration, abolished racial discrimination, tried to lay
the foundations of an educational system, sent young Mulattoes
and Negroes to France to be educated so as to return and be able
to govern. He treated the whites with exceptional consideration
and courtesy, so much so that the black laborers began to lose
confidence in him. Too confident of his influence over the blacks,
he sacrificed his popularity to please the French.

But the political situation in France had changed for the
worse. The revolution had stabilized itself under Bonaparte. And
Bonaparte sought to restore slavery. He sent an expedition under his brother-in-law Leclerc which finally amounted to nearly
60,000 men. Toussaint vacillated at first, then fought and finally
came to terms. Captured by a trick he was sent to France, and
died in an Alpine prison. But as soon as Bonaparte's plans for the
restoration of slavery and all the discrimination of the old regime
became known, the population, which bad been partially de-
ceived by Leclerc's false proclamations, revolted. Dessalines, one
of Toussaint's lieutenants, had by this time seen what Toussaint
never saw, that only independence could guarantee freedom. The

Mulattoes, who had previously supported Bonaparte, joined the blacks, and together they fought a desperate war of independence. To win they had almost to destroy the island. France, from casualties in battle and fever, suffered the loss of over 50,000 men. The cruelties practiced by the French during the last stages of the civil war exceeded in barbarism the worst of the old slavery days. Dessalines, uncultured and lacking Toussaint's genius, led his people with a ruthlessness quite equal to that of the French.

The attitude of the whites toward changes in the San Domingo regime throws a valuable light on race prejudice. Before the revolution Negroes were so despised that white women undressed before them as one undresses today before a dog or a cat. Ten years after, when former slaves were now ruling the country, most of the whites accepted the new regime, fraternized with the ex-slave generals and dined at their tables; while the white women, members of some of the proudest families of the French aristocracy, threw themselves recklessly at the black dictator, sent him locks of hair, keepsakes, passionate letters, etc. To the laboring Negroes, however, they showed as much of their old hostility as they dared. When the Leclerc expedition came, the whites rushed to join it, and took a leading part in the gladiatorial shows where dogs ate living Negroes, etc. But when they saw that Leclerc's expedition was doomed to defeat, they disentangled themselves from it and turned again to the blacks. Dessalines, the new dictator, declared the island independent, but promised them their properties. This was enough for them. When the French commanders were about to evacuate the island they offered the white colonists places on the boats. The colonists refused, being quite content to continue living under blacks who were no longer French even in allegiance: the San Domingo blacks gave their island its old Carib name, Haiti, to emphasize the break with France.

But the British and the Americans, themselves the greatest slave-holders in the world, were all for the victory of the blacks in order to drive out the French. All through Leclerc's campaign the British and American newspapers cursed the French and praised Toussaint and the blacks. That Frenchmen should remain in the island did not suit them. While Dessalines, who hated the whites for their accumulated treacheries, wanted to kill as many as possible, Christophe and Clairveaux, his two trusted lieutenants, disapproved, and the great bulk of the people wanted no more bloodshed. But Cathcart, an English agent in San Domingo, told Dessalines that the British would neither trade with him nor accord him their protection unless every Frenchman were killed. Not long after the French were massacred. M. Camille Guy tells the story and gives his original sources in pamphlet No. 3 of the *Bulletin de geographic*, published in Paris in 1898. There too he gives details of the presents that were sent to Dessalines for his coronation from London in a British cruiser and from America. Needless to say, in most books on this subject, black Dessalines bears the sole responsibility for this massacre.

The success of the San Domingo blacks killed the West Indian slave-trade and slavery. France hoped for many years that she would regain the colony. The Haitians let her know that they would resist to the last man and burn everything to the ground. France therefore resigned herself to the loss and with the removal of San Domingo from the West Indian trade, abolition of the slave-trade in 1807 and of slavery in 1834 followed. The English planters fought hard but history was against them. The revolution in France in 1848, during its short-lived span of success, abolished slavery in the French colonies.

The San Domingo revolution is the only successful Negro revolt, and therefore the reasons for that success must be noted. First the blacks themselves fought magnificently and glowing tributes have been paid to them by their opponents. But many had fought well before and have fought well since. They were fortunate in that they had had time to organize themselves as soldiers. And this was due to the fact that they not only received inspiration from the revolution in France but between 1794 and 1797 had active support from revolutionary France. Such supplies and reinforcements as did actually arrive were comparatively small, but were directed toward assisting and not retarding the slave revolution. This was the decisive factor. The international situation also helped them. But the conflict between Britain and France, then between France on the one hand and Spain on the other was also the result of the revolution. During the last campaign, at a very critical moment, the declaration of war between France and Britain, after the short interval which followed the Treaty of Amiens, made the victory of the San Domingo blacks inevitable. But the blacks maneuvered with great skill. The Spaniards, and in the later stages after their defeat, the British, both offered terms to the blacks with the secret intention of turning upon them afterward and restoring slavery. Maitland, the British general, say so very clearly in his letter to the Foreign Secretary, Dundas, dated December 26, 1798, and preserved in the Public Record Office. But Toussaint never compromised himself with the British. While taking from them as much assistance as was convenient, he refused any entangling alliances. He thus made the most skillful use of imperialist contradictions when revolutionary France, crushed, was no longer able to assist him.

There remains to be noted a certain aspect of the struggle which though derivative is yet of extreme importance. During the revolutionary period the blacks fought under the slogans of liberty and equality. They embraced the revolutionary doctrine, they thought in republican terms. The result was that these slaves, lacking education, half-savage, and degraded in their slavery as only centuries of slavery can degrade, achieved a liberality in social aspiration and an elevation of political thought equivalent to anything similar that took place in France. Hundreds of Toussaint's letters, proclamations, etc., are preserved, some in the national archives in France, others in San Domingo. Papers of contemporary blacks and Mulattoes also exist. Christophe and Dessalines, who shared the leadership with Toussaint, were quite illiterate, slaves sprung from the ranks. But they and their fellow officers not only acted but spoke and dictated like highly-trained modern revolutionaries.

Some examples should be given. All the blacks did not join the French. Some remained with the Spanish rulers of Spanish San Domingo. The leader of these, full of racial pride, rejected the overtures of the French and told Laveaux, the French Commander, that he would only believe in his pretended equality when he saw Monsieur Laveaux and gentlemen of his quality giving their daughters in marriage to Negroes. But the blacks who were republican had the utmost scorn for the blacks who were royalist. Witness the following proclamation in reply to overtures made on behalf of the Spanish authorities by the blacks who supported royalism.

> We are republicans and, in consequence, free by natural right. It can only be Kings whose very name expresses what is most vile and low, who dared to arrogate the right of reducing to slavery men made like themselves, whom nature had made free.
>
> The King of Spain furnishes you abundantly with arms and ammunition. Use them to tighten your chains. . . . As for us, we have no need for more than stones and sticks to make you dance the Carmapole. . . .
>
> You have received commissions and you have guarantees. Guard your liveries and your parchments. One day they will serve you as the fastidious titles of our former aristocrats served them. If the King of the French who drags his misery from court to court has need of slaves to assist him in his magnificence, let him go seek it among other Kings who count as many slaves as they have subjects.

When Toussaint L'Ouverture began to suspect in 1797 that the French Government was now the representative of forces which might ultimately aim at the restoration of slavery, he addressed to them a letter which seems to come straight from the pen of Mirabeau, Danton or Robespierre, instead of from a slave who dictated in the local patois and then had his thoughts written and rewritten until his secretaries had achieved the form which he desired.

> Do they think that men who have been able to enjoy the blessing of liberty will calmly see it snatched away? They supported their chains only so long as they did not know any condition of life more happy than that of slavery. But today when they have left it, if they had a thousand lives they would sacrifice them all rather than be forced into slavery again. But no, the same hand which has broken our chains will not enslave us anew. France will not revoke her principles, she will

not withdraw from us the greatest of her benefits. She will protect us from all our enemies; she will not permit her sublime morality to be perverted, those principles which do her most honor to be destroyed, her most beautiful achievement to be degraded, her Decree of the 16th Pluviose which so honors humanity to be revoked. *But if, to re-establish slavery in San Domingo, this was done, then I declare to you it would be to attempt the impossible: we have known how to face dangers to obtain our liberty, we shall know how to brave death to maintain it.* (Italics his own.)

This, Citizen Directors, is the morale of the people of San Domingo, those are the principles that they transmit to you by me.

My own you know. It is sufficient to renew, my hand in yours, the oath that I have made, to cease to live before gratitude dies in my heart, before I cease to be faithful to France and to my duty, before the god of liberty is profaned and sullied by the liberticides, before they can snatch from my hands that sword, those arms, which France confided to me "for the defense of its rights and those of humanity, for the triumph of liberty and equality."

Race prejudice was rampant before the revolution and blacks and Mulattoes hated each other as much as did the blacks and whites. Yet by 1799 when the civil war was about to begin between the blacks of the North and West and the Mulattoes of the South, a civil war based on the different social interests of the two classes, Rigaud the Mulatto leader, instead of emphasizing the difference in color as Mulattoes always did before the revolution, now defended himself with moving passion against the conception that he was hostile to Toussaint, the Commander-in-Chief, because Toussaint was a Negro.

Indeed, if I had reached the stage where I would not wish to obey a black, if I had the stupid presumption to believe that I am above such obedience, on what grounds could I claim obedience from the whites? What a grievous example would I be giving to those placed under my orders? Besides, is there so great a difference between the color of the Commander-in-Chief and mine? Is it a tint of color, more or less dark, which instills principles of philosophy or gives merit to an individual? . . . I have consecrated my life to the defense of the blacks. From the beginning of the revolution I have braved all for the cause of liberty. I have not betrayed my principles and I shall never do so. Besides, I am too much a believer in the Rights of Man to think that there is one color in nature superior to another. I know a man only as a man.

The revolution under the encouragement of the French revolutionaries seemed to have created a new nation. The great tragedy of San Domingo was that as the revolution in France retreated before reaction, the old slave-owners regained influence and harassed the exhausted blacks.

2

The Old United States

The revolts in the United States follow the same line as those in the West Indies before 1789, constant ill-organized uprisings which are always crushed with comparative ease.

A typical revolt was that which took place at Stono, a plantation some twenty miles to the West of Carolina, in September 1739. A few score of slaves killed the two guards of a magazine, armed themselves and set out for the Edisto river. Other Negroes joined them, they marched with colors displayed, drums beating, shouting for liberty, and killing and burning all in their path. They killed about twenty-five whites, but spared one who was a good man and kind to his slaves. After some miles of this destruction they stopped to rest, but were surprised by their white owners who had followed in pursuit. They fought bravely, but they were defeated, and most of them were either shot in battle, hanged, or gibbeted alive. That is the theme on which the variations were played in state after state in America as in island after island in the West Indies. The slaves gained nothing by these revolts. No attempt is made to treat them more kindly. Instead revolts are savagely repressed and the severity of slave legislation increased.

Yet these American revolts between 1670 and 1860 follow certain laws. This of 1739 was one of a series which took place in South Carolina between 1737 and 1740, a period of grave economic difficulties. There is imperialist intrigue at work. Spain still had colonies in America and the Spaniards were encouraging these American slaves to rebel. Many of the Negroes had been captured in Angola, and being Catholic, were attracted to the Spaniards. When the revolting Negroes set out for the Edisto river, they intended to follow it to its mouth, which was in Spanish territory. Finally the Negroes outnumbered the whites four to one in this state. Yet despite these favorable circumstances the revolt seems to have neglected the thousands of slaves who, it may be presumed, were not unwilling to join. While their masters lived in constant terror, the Negroes themselves seemed unconscious of their revolutionary potentialities when organized on an extensive scale.

The San Domingo revolution and its success dominated the minds of Negroes in the West Indies and America for the next generation. In America, where the slaves had periodically revolted from the very beginning of slavery, San Domingo inspired a series of fresh revolts during the succeeding twenty years. Documented accounts of these American slave revolts have appeared in the United States. In 1795 a revolt in Louisiana failed to take place owing to a quarrel as to the method. But this revolt is notable because an important feature now appears which seems to have been the direct result of the revolutionary ferment of the age: there were whites in alliance with the Negroes from the very beginning. Five years afterward, in 1800, there took place the well-known revolt headed by the Negro slave Gabriel, in Virginia. The white authorities, fortunately for them, heard about it before the uprising actually began and were thus able to take precautions. About a thousand slaves, armed with clubs and swords, which they had been making since the last harvest, gathered six miles away from the town of Richmond. But a tremendous storm flooded the rivers, lore down bridges and made it impossible to conduct military operations. The revolt ended as always in failure and bloody suppression. Yet Gabriel and his followers were slave revolutionaries above the average. They intended to spare Frenchmen because the Frenchmen were associated in their minds with liberty, equality and fraternity. They were also going to spare Quakers and Methodists because these were consistently opposed to slavery. They confidently expected the poorer whites to join them. After the fore-doomed defeat, Gabriel was captured, tried and executed. It is not known how many Negroes were concerned, but the numbers suggested varied between 2,000 and 10,000.

Despite the accidents which overtook this revolt at its beginning, it is impossible to see what other result but defeat awaited it. It had no support among powerful revolutionary elements in the country. It had no support abroad. Similar failures awaited the plots in Virginia and North Carolina in 1801–2. For these, however, we have clear evidence that the poor whites of the districts had definitely allied themselves with the Negroes. This is the recruiting speech of one of the revolting Negroes: "I have taken it on myself to let the country be at liberty, this lies upon my mind for a long time. Mind men I have told you a great deal I have joined with both black and white which is the common men or poor white people, Mulattoes will join with me to help free the country, although they are free already. I have got eight or ten white men to lead me in the fight on the magazine, they will be before me and hand out guns, powder, pistols, shot and other things that will answer the purpose . . . black men I mean to lose my life in this if they will take it."

There were risings in 1811 and again in 1816, but even as late as 1822 in Virginia, one Denmark Vesey, a free Negro, attempted to lead a revolt which was partially inspired by San Domingo. Vesey based his attempt on his readings of the Bible, but he also had the San Domingo revolution in mind, for he wrote to the rulers of Haiti, telling them of his plans and asking for aid. Despite his religious outlook, or because of it, all who opposed the rising were to be killed. The numbers involved were said to have been between 6,000 and 9,000, and some of his supporters came from as far away as eighty miles. The insurrection was betrayed, probably by that mischievous type—the house-slave who was kindly treated by his master and wore his cast-off clothes.

The last important American revolt was Nat Turner's, born out of the anti-slavery agitation which was to end in the abolition of slavery in the British colonies. Mexico abolished slavery in 1829 and in this period, right through the West Indies and Spanish America, there was slave revolt after slave revolt. Turner's revolt was not very wide in scope. An intelligent and gifted man, he took his inspiration from the Bible. In February 1831 about seventy Negroes, some of them mounted, covered an area of about twenty miles and killed about sixty women and children. They were ultimately defeated by hundreds of state troops. Turner was caught and hanged.

So far, Turner's revolt was commonplace. But this revolt had an effect out of all proportion to its size. Though there are reports of slave conspiracies and of plots all over the Southern states for the next thirty years, nothing on a large scale seems to have been attempted. On the other hand at the time of the Turner revolt the Southern slave owners realized that the unrest "was not confined to the slaves." Henceforward the fear of unity between the blacks and the poor whites drove the South to treat with great severity any opposition to slavery in the South from whatever source it came. A rigid censorship was instituted. In the years before the American Civil War the turmoil among the slaves was widespread all over the South. Their chance came, however, not from the poor whites of the South but from the economic and political necessities of the Northern whites.

3

The Civil War

Before we consider the course of emancipation in America, let us see what the Negroes were to be emancipated from. In 1860, little more than seventy-five years ago, Negro slavery was still widespread in the Southern states of America. We know what slavery was like during the eighteenth century. It had not changed much in the last half of the nineteenth.

Here is a case that reads as if it came straight from San Domingo, Barbados or British Guiana in 1749.

> The Negro was tied to a tree and whipped with switches. When Souther became fatigued with the labor of whipping, he called upon a Negro man of his and made him "cob" Sam with a single.

He also made a Negro woman of his help to 'cob' him. And, after "cobbing" and whipping, he applied fire to the body of his slave, about his back, belly and private parts. He then caused him to be washed down with hot water in which pods of *red pepper* had been steeped. The Negro was also tied to a log, and to the bedpost, with ropes, which choked him, and he was kicked and stamped upon by Souther. This sort of punishment was continued and repeated until the Negro died under its affliction.

The records of the time tell the same tale of burnings, mutilations, etc., as in the West Indies 150 years before.

Every slave-owner did not spend every hour of the day beating and torturing his slaves. But few of his neighbors cared if he did, and if he tortured them, it was done so infrequently that it occasioned no surprise in those who saw it. In this respect 1860 was not very different from 1660. Gladstone and *The London Times* both supported the slave-owners against the North in the American Civil War.

In this very period, Governor Eyre of Jamaica, without the slightest justification, authorized a murderous persecution of Negroes who had revolted under great provocation and had behaved with great moderation. Maroons were called in, who dashed out the brains of children and ripped open pregnant women; while the more civilized Provost Marshal Ramsay shot victims with his own band and flogged victims until their flesh bespattered the ground. Nearly 500 Negroes were killed and thousands of Negroes were whipped, sometimes with a cat in the strings of which piano-wire was interwoven; as many as two hundred lashes each were administered. Britain was divided, Carlyle leading the defense of Eyre, who was retired on pension. Coming as it did just at the time of the American Civil War, this incident is related here, so that the cruelty of Americans to their slaves might be seen in reasonable perspective.

Obviously the conscience of mankind or growing enlightenment was not going to abolish Negro slavery in America. These forces in the heart of man had not abolished slavery for 250 years. Why should they suddenly be potent in 1850?

First of all, as we have seen, the Negro was no docile animal. He revolted continuously. By 1850 he had changed his tactics. For over a generation before the outbreak of the Civil War, the bolder slaves of the South sought freedom by flight to the North, whose economic structure had no need of slavery. In the South, the mountaineers of North Carolina, Kentucky and Tennessee had no need of slaves. They formed anti-slavery societies, and Christian and Liberal revolutionaries assisted fugitive slaves to escape. These and some bold Negroes organized the famous Underground Railway to assist escaping slaves. By various special routes slaves were conducted from the South to the Northern states, where they were free. Thousands of blacks gained their freedom in this way. Bravest and most famous of these underground guides was the Negro, Harriet Tubman. Born a slave, she escaped, but rifle in hand she devoted her life to assisting others to actual freedom by means of the Underground. The Southern owners offered a reward of 40,000 dollars for her capture, but she used to penetrate into the very heart of the South in order to achieve her aims. Not only slaves but free Negroes took part in all this agitation and organization. When John Brown made his famous raid there were Negroes with him, some of whom lost their lives in the fighting, and others at the hands of Southern law. The agitation of the abolitionists, the sensational escapes by the Underground Railway, the ferment among the Negroes, all helped to focus public attention on slavery. But long before the Civil War the great issues at stake were becoming clear.

The South had dominated the Federal Legislation for more than half a century, but with the increasing industrial expansion of the North, that domination was now in danger. Both North and South were expanding westward. Should the new states be based on slavery as the South wanted or on free capitalism as the North wanted? This was not a moral question. Victory here meant increasing control of the legislature by the victors. The moment the North were strong enough they decreed that there was to be no further extension of slave territory. Nothing else remained for the South but war. Had the Southerners won, their reactionary method of production and the backward civilization based upon it would have dominated the United States. No won-der Karl Marx hailed the Civil War as the greatest event of the age. He was not concerned with the morality or immorality of slavery. What he could see so early was the grandeur of the civilization which lay before the States with the victory of the North. Thus if the Civil War resulted in the abolition of slavery it was not fought for the benefit of the slaves.

Yet Negro slavery seemed the very basis of American capitalism. Slavery made cotton king; cotton became the very life food of British industries, it built up New England factories. This accounts for not merely the support given to the South by Conservatives but even by certain British Liberals. The protagonists had no illusions. Lincoln once told a Massachusetts audience cheerfully, "I have heard you have abolitionists here. We have a few in Illinois, and we shot one the other day." Lincoln said openly that to save the Union he would free all the slaves, or free some, or free none.

What we are really witnessing here is not that sudden change in the conscience of mankind so beloved of romantic and reactionary historians, but the climax of a gradual transformation of world economy. Where formerly landed property had dominated, the French Revolution marks the beginning of the social and political domination of the industrial bourgeoisie. It began in the French Revolution, in Britain its outstanding dates are the Reform Bill of 1832 and the Repeal of the Corn Laws in 1846, and it reached its culmination with the Civil War in America. The process worked itself out blindly and irrationally. In territories like San Domingo and later Brazil, where new and rich lands cried out for cultivation, the slave remained profitable for years. But we can see today that once capitalism had begun to throw off feudal shackles, slavery was doomed. The millions of slaves were not only ignorant and backward, with a low productivity of labor. Their potential consumption as free men widened the scope of the market. Thus the San Domingo revolution, the abolition of the slave-trade in 1807, the emancipation of the slaves in 1833, and emancipation during the Civil War in America, all these events are but component parts of a single historic process. However confused, dishonest, selfish, idealistic or sincere might be the minds of the abolitionists, they were in the last analysis the agents of the economic necessities of the new age, translated into social and political, sometimes, even, religious terms.

Lincoln long maintained his attitude. It was the pressure of war which forced him to accept emancipation. The South were using Negroes to build fortifications, roads, etc., all the important labor of their armies. Where at first be feared a slave revolt which would weaken his political position in the North, he now saw the necessity of at least using slaves for labor purposes. Refugees poured over to the Northern forces and Lincoln tried to get some of them dispatched to Africa, to Haiti and other territories outside America. He was at that time considering a scheme of gradual abolition based upon compensation.

But the Negro refugees were establishing themselves in the army as capable teamsters, mechanics, and general workers. They were industrious and loyal. The South was proving more difficult to conquer than had at first been thought, and the Negroes would have to be used as soldiers. In 1862 Congress declared that after January 1, 1863, all slaves in rebel territory were free. Northern generals were urging Lincoln to enlist Negroes, and one had already taken the step on his own initiative. The South formed corps of free Negroes who were fighting in its army. Thus Lincoln's objections were finally overcome by the necessity of events. Before the end of 1865 four Negro regiments were in the field and at the end of the war, three years afterward, 178,875 Negroes had been enrolled in the Northern army. Seventy-five commissions were given, but the Negroes were commanded chiefly by white men. They were discriminated against, being treated as less than the equals of whites. Two regiments refused to accept their pay until it was made equal to that of white men, and one sergeant was court-martialed and shot because he made his company stack arms before the captain's hut as a protest against discrimination. White troops often used them for fatigue duty. This unfair treatment affected the morale of the blacks, who were often sullen and insubordinate. But of their military quality there was never any question. They defeated some of the crack Southern troops, men who had formerly owned them. Surgeon Seth Rogers said of his soldiers that braver men never lived, and Colonel T.W. Higginson declared that "it would have been madness to attempt with the bravest white troops what he successfully accomplished with the black": the white troops were not fighting for freedom. Brave as were these blacks, there was nothing naive about them. "They met death coolly, bravely; nor rashly did they expose themselves, but all were steady and obedient to orders." Lincoln himself admitted that but for the assistance given by the Negroes, the North might have lost. He spoke more wisely than he knew. Negro scholarship in America has conducted investigations, which tend to show that not only the Negro soldiers but the Negroes left behind in the South played a decisive part in the outcome. In the first years of the war the Southern blacks took the side of their masters. They knew them, they did not know the North, and as both were for the maintenance of slavery the difference between them was of no importance. But after the proclamation of emancipation, the news spread and it is claimed that there took place a sort of general strike, an immense sabotage, which helped to bring the South to its knees. Slavery degrades, but under the shock of great events like a revolution, slaves of centuries seem able to conduct themselves with the bravery and discipline of men who have been free a thousand years.

The American blacks were far more indebted to the political conflicts between North and South America for their freedom than the San Domingo blacks had been to the French Revolution. They were only four million, a minority, even in the South. They were tied indissolubly to America. What was now to become of them?

The Negroes themselves knew what they wanted—the land—and had they been strong enough to take it, or had the Northern capitalists the wisdom to give it to them, the possibilities opened up both for the Negro and American capitalism would have been immense. The bourgeois revolution against feudalism is only economically complete when the peasants have the land. It was so in France in 1789 and in Russia in 1917. Peasants today are politically alert as never before.

The Negroes tried to take the land. They had fought with an instinctive confidence that it was going to be theirs, so much so that much of the idleness and discontent in certain areas after the Civil War could be traced to the fact that they had not got what they expected. In certain areas they actually seized the land

and refused to return it. The Negro soldiers and the militia were trained to arms, they and their allies secured large quantities of ammunition, and in the latter part of 1865 the South lived in fear of a slave insurrection. The proposal was actually made to oppose the return of confiscated property and substitute instead a scheme for dividing the estates of the leading rebels into forty-acre plots for each freed man. The rest would be sold to pay off the national debt and fifty dollars would be given to each homestead as a start.

Revolutionary as these proposals were, yet nine-tenths of the population of the South would have been untouched. But Congress, though busy expropriating the farmers of the West and even the South for the benefit of the railroad and mining companies, would not touch Southern property for the benefit of the Negroes. It would have meant the creation of a body of peasant proprietors for whom co-operative and similar schemes would have been comparatively easy, it would have resulted in a great extension, of the internal "market," and the Negro question would never have been the problem that it is today in America. This revolution could easily have been accomplished in the early days after the Civil War. The Southerners were too cowed to resist, the sporadic efforts of the Negroes only needed coordination. Why was the opportunity missed? First, because the peasants in a revolution have to seize the land. Only the Jacobins, as late as 1793, ratified the seizure in France. The Kerensky government in Russia could go no further than an elaborate land law, and the peasants had to wait for the Bolsheviks to encourage and legalize the seizure. Only a revolution in which the poor were the driving force would have held out its hand to the blacks and made common cause of its own objectives and land for the blacks. There was no such revolution in America. What the dominant American bourgeoisie did, however, is as revealing of the true nature of American race prejudice as the behavior of the San Domingo whites during the black revolution. The war had divided the Northern bourgeoisie into the small men on the one hand and on the other, the bankers, the magnates of iron and steel and the railways, linking themselves into great corporations. Monopoly capitalism was on its way. But it was as yet small. In a new country its control of propaganda, organs of publicity, etc., was not sufficient to ensure its control of elections. The small capitalists would outnumber the big capitalists and gain control of the government. Writing in the *American Mercury* of April 1938, a Southerner has shown that the huge patriarchal estates of the South are a tenacious legend with no foundation in fact. Most of the Southern slave-owners were farmers on a not very large scale. There was also a small capitalist class growing in the South. A combination between these and their brethren in the North would be fatal to the monopolists. By illegally excluding representatives of the Southern States from the legislature, the big bourgeoisie passed legislation to ensure their predominance and enfranchised the Negroes in order to use these votes against their white rivals in the South. They then dispatched special agents, the carpet-baggers, to pose as the friends of the Negro and to manipulate the Negro vote in their favor.

Thus the North did not allow race prejudice against the Negro to impede its wishes, accepted the fact that he was needed to help hold the South in control, and cooperated politically with him. The Southern states were offered the choice of military government or universal manhood suffrage "without regard to color, race or previous condition of servitude." They were thus trapped either way. Some of the states accepted the Negro voter, others refused, among them Virginia, Georgia and Texas. Between 1868 and 1872 certain states were governed by whites and blacks, many of the blacks being newly-emancipated slaves.

The idea that the Negroes dominated is wholly false. Only twenty-three Negroes served in Congress from 1868 to 1895. Many Negro state officials were illiterate; in certain state legislatures more than half the Negro members could scarcely read or write. Yet there were among them many capable men. There is no evidence to prove that they were more than usually corrupt or rapacious. The Northerners who entered these Southern governments and plundered them were potent sources of corruption. The black officials naturally sided with Northerners against the old slave-owners. When in a few years the Southern states were restored to Southern control, in nearly every state the white officers in control of the funds defaulted. But no exposure was made of this. In another generation, Northern monopoly capitalism had America in its grasp. It left the Negro to his fate, and the South turned on him. Landless, his Northern collaborators gone, he was whipped back to an existence bordering on servitude.

Yet despite the inevitable ignorance and backwardness, the few years during which the Negroes were associated with the government of certain Southern states marked the high watermark of progressive legislation in the South. Little publicity is given to the things they helped to do. "They obeyed the Constitution and annulled the bonds of states, counties and cities which were issued to carry on the War of Rebellion and maintain armies in the field against the Union. They instituted a public school system in the realm where public schools had been unknown. They opened the ballot-box and jury-box to thousands of white men who had been debarred from them by lack of earthly possessions. They introduced Home Rule in the South. They abolished the whipping post, the branding-iron, the stocks, and other barbarous forms of punishment which, up to that time, prevailed. They reduced capital felonies from about twenty to two or three. In an age of extravagance, they were extravagant in the sums appropriated for public works. In all that time no man's right of person was invaded under the forms of law. Every Democrat's life, home, fireside and business were safe. No man obstructed any white man's way to the ballot-box, interfered with his freedom or boycotted him on account of his political faith." It was the policy of a people poor and backward seeking to establish a community where all, black and white, could live in amity and freedom. It deserves to be remembered.

4

Revolts in Africa

For four centuries the African in Africa had had to suffer from the raids of the slave dealers and the dislocation of African civilization that had been caused thereby. America continued with the slave-trade until the end of the Civil War, but whereas in 1789 San Domingo alone was taking 40,000 slaves a year, between 1808 and 1860, the Southern states of North America took only 200,000. Other nations of Europe and the Arabs on the East coast continued the trade. Actual colonies, however, were comparatively few in Africa. There was, of course. Cape Colony and the districts beyond, and colonies in West Africa which were on the whole little more than trading stations. In the middle of the nineteenth century Disraeli referred to colonies as damned millstones around the necks of the British people. As we have said it is unlikely that more than one-tenth of Africa was in European hands. But in the 1880s began the intensive rivalry of European imperialisms for colonies as the sources of raw materials, for markets and spheres of influence. By the end of the nineteenth century, less than one-tenth of Africa remained in the hands of Africans themselves. This rapid change could not fail to produce a series of revolts, which have never ceased.

Before we consider the actual revolts, it is necessary to see, briefly, what the Negro is revolting against. European colonization is broadly speaking of two types, the first, as in South Africa, the two Rhodesias and Kenya, where it is possible for Europeans to settle and remain; the second in British West Africa, where the European is for the most part official and trader, does not look upon the colony as his home and does not settle there in large numbers.

In areas like the Union of South Africa, the Rhodesias and Kenya, the white settlers have to force the native to leave his own work and interests in order to labor for them in mine or plantation. The method they adopt is to tax him by means of a poll tax. The Negro, though perhaps quite comfortably placed according to his own wishes and needs, must have money to pay this tax, which compels him therefore to seek employment with European masters, on whatever conditions these choose to lay down. Hence the wages of four pence a day in Kenya and 15 shillings a month in the copper mines of Rhodesia. The Europeans also take the best land and herd the natives in areas which are not only difficult to cultivate but too small for their most elementary needs. In the Union of South Africa, for instance, about 2,000,000 whites own about eighty percent of the land, while over 6,000,000 natives own ten percent. The rest is Crown land, that is to say, at the disposal of the white government. Obviously this state of affairs can only be maintained by a social and political regime based on terror.

The natives are made to carry passes which they must produce on request; a pass if they are out later than nine o'clock, a pass to show that their tax has been paid, a pass from their employer, fingerprints for identification—in the Union of South Africa there are a dozen passes of one kind or another which the Negro may have to carry. A Negro who has a profession is given an exemption pass, which absolves him from the necessity of carrying these other passes. But any native policeman is able to ask him for this exemption pass, and arrest him on the spot if it is not produced at once. Negroes, whatever their status, whatever their appearance, are debarred from frequenting all public places of business or entertainment frequented by whites. In places like the post office, there are two counters, one for whites and one for blacks.

What does the native get in return? After four hundred years of European occupation, there are not half-a-dozen native doctors in South Africa. Over three-quarters of the native population are almost entirely without education. The education supplied to the rest is officially admitted to be of the poorest quality. Far from making a gradual, if slow, political progress, the natives of the Cape have recently been deprived of the franchise, a relic of more liberal days. They are debarred by law from being even skilled laborers, as tyrannical and demoralizing a piece of legislation as has been passed in any country during the last hundred years.

In the mines they receive one-eighth of the wages of the white miner. In ancient territories like the Union of South Africa, or in more modern areas as Rhodesia and Kenya, the method is exactly the same, with slight local variations. While politicians in Britain speak of trusteeship, South African white leaders and officials in Rhodesia and Kenya periodically state quite unequivocally that Africa is to be run for the benefit of the whites and the Negro must make up his mind to know his place and keep it.

In West Africa the situation is somewhat different. There, over large areas, the Negroes were guaranteed their land by law, at a time when it seemed unlikely that Europeans would ever need it. European capital, of course, dominates. But the racial discrimination is not nearly so acute as in the South and in the East of Africa, and the conflict between the Negroes and their rulers is more strictly economic and political than it is in the Cape or Kenya.

French Equatorial Africa and the Belgian Congo form two areas to some degree different from those described above. In a

French colony, a Negro who by education or military service becomes a French citizen, is given all privileges, and is governed by
the laws which apply to white men. He can become a high official in the government service, or a general in the French army.
During the war Petain's Chief of Staff at Verdun was a Negro.
Commandant Avenol, who was in charge of the air defense of
Paris from 1914 to 1918 with ten thousand men under him, including British and white American aviators, was a Martinique
Negro. At the present moment the Governor of Guadeloupe is
a black man. These men, it is true, are from the old West Indian
colonies. But there are Africans in the service, and it is admitted
that promotion is open to them on practically the same terms
as whites. There have been Africans, deputies in the Chamber,
who have become Cabinet Ministers. After the war the French
issued a serious warning to Americans in Paris who tried to
introduce American race prejudice, and it is noteworthy that
these Americans who cannot tolerate the sight of a Negro in
an American restaurant, learned in Paris to admit him and his
white girl friends into an American bar: Briand told them that
he would close down the bar if they didn't. This is a valuable feature of French civilization and disposes of many illusions, carefully cultivated in America and Britain, about Negro incapacity
and racial incompatibility. But imperialism remains imperialism.
During the last twenty years the population of French Congo has
declined by more than six millions, and the French have as black
a record in Africa as any other imperialist nation.

In the Belgian Congo the Negro has certain privileges; for
example, he is allowed to occupy important posts on the railways,
which is forbidden to him in South Africa. Thus Negroes run
trains to the border of the Belgian colonies where South African
whites take them over. Yet the Belgian attitude is less liberal than
the French. No African who has spent more than six months
abroad is allowed to return to the Congo, and the severity of the
forced labor regulations is such that when the company which
owns the sugar plantations of Moabeke built a railway, almost the
entire male population of the district was worked to death. This
is in no way exceptional. French and Belgians have an evil reputation in the Congo for cold-blooded cruelty. As in the days of

slavery in the West Indian colonies, the European colonizing nations claim superiority to each other. But an African in Eritrea is no worse off under Italian Fascism than an African in the Congo under democratic Belgium, or a Rhodesian copper miner.

The Old Colonies

Let us begin with revolts in one of the oldest colonies on the West Coast, Sierra Leone. The Negroes in the actual colony are some of the most advanced in education and should be grouped with those of the West Indies rather than with those in Central or Eastern Africa. Freetown, the capital, for instance, was until recent years a municipality. The hinterland is, however, a protectorate where the less developed Africans are governed by the method of indirect rule.

At the end of the last century there were two Negro communities, one with its own press, barristers-at-law, doctors and other intelligentsia, and on the other hand the natives in the interior, the new Africa and the old. These two communities were divided. Those with generations of British education had an outlook similar to that of the majority of Negroes in the West Indies: they regarded the African tribes as barbarous and uncivilized. The African tribes looked upon these Europeanized blacks as black white men. In 1898 a revolt burst in the protectorate. The natives resented the paying of the poll tax and the Mendi, a famous fighting tribe, had a special grievance of their own: they objected to corporal punishment. So much did they oppose it, that they would not send their children to the missionary schools where the missionaries sometimes beat them. The tribes completely wiped out some battalions of West Indian blacks who were sent against them, and it is claimed by Negroes who were in Sierra Leone at the time that certain white battalions were also completely destroyed. The great massacres of government soldiers took place at Sherbro and Mofeno. The revolt was of course put down, many hundreds of natives being killed. The insurgents killed not only white and black soldiers and every missionary they could put their hands on, but also certain of the Europeanized blacks as well. They looked upon all of these as members of one exploiting, arrogant group. The war, however, has marked the beginning of a change.

The conflict of capital and labor is intensified by the fact that capital is usually white and labor black; this in a continent where the whites have always sought to justify their economic exploitation and social privilege by the mere fact of difference of color. The class conflict, bitter enough in countries where the population is homogeneous in color, has an added bitterness in Africa, which has been strengthened by the growth of nationalism among the post-war intelligentsia. The politically conscious minority increasingly realize that their future is with the developing Africans rather than with the European traders. Further, they are Africans in Africa—not the descendants of Africans, as in the West Indies. The result is a growing solidarity between the blacks, chiefly workers in the colony and the more untutored Africans in the protectorate. Black politicians in the colony attribute the ill-feeling in 1898 to white propaganda aimed at dividing potential allies, and they have common ground in that they are Negroes in a continent where to be black is to be inferior. It is against this background that we must see more recent movements in Sierra Leone and Gambia.

In 1919, there was a railway strike in Sierra Leone. The railway workers attempted to get other workers to join with them and were joined by over 2,000 police striking for higher wages. In 1926 there was another railway strike and the workers again attempted to make the strike general and to win over the police. The strikers showed an extraordinary militancy. They removed the rails in front of the manager's train. They attacked it with sticks. They removed or loosened the rails on curves or steep banks and at the approach to a bridge, pulled down telegraph poles and cut wires to prevent telegraphic communication with the protectorate. In the words of the Governor, "it was a revolt against the state by its servants." The municipality supported the strike and the native press hinted at rebellion, whereupon the Governor suppressed the municipality. We have here a very sharp division between the African laborers and the employers in industry, mostly white.

In Gambia, a colony that is usually grouped with Sierra Leone, the seamen are organized and in 1929 a sailors' strike lasted forty days and then grew into a general strike. At the same time, the farmers, hostile over the low prices paid for their products, carried on strenuous agitation. The people were fired upon and nearly fifty were wounded. After three weeks of the general strike, the Colonial Secretary addressed a letter to the Union seeking arbitration. The Government finally combined with the employers to defeat the strike. This was not a revolt, but shows the capacity for organized action which has developed in these older colonies, while an outbreak which took place in Sierra Leone in February 1931, shows the possibility of revolts infinitely more dangerous than any that have hitherto taken place. Hundreds of Negroes from the protectorate, led by an armed battalion of fifty men, invaded the Kambia district. The leader was Hahilara, a Negro Muslim leader who had converted thousands of natives to Mohammedanism, with which he united anti-imperialism. Hahilara called upon the peasants to refuse to pay taxes and to drive away the British officials. He demanded that all Crown lands in the protectorate should be confiscated and divided among the landless peasants. This was social revolution. Hahilara's agitation had widespread support. The Government attempted to arrest him, but the Negroes threatened to kill all Europeans who entered their territory. Government soldiers invaded the territory, and Hahilara was defeated and killed. But Captain H. J. Holmes, the officer commanding the British troops, was also killed. Hundreds of native huts were burnt to the ground and the rising was suppressed.

Yet perhaps the most significant feature of the revolt was the attitude of the Negro press in the colony, which emphasized the grievances of the insurgents in the protectorate. Sympathy among the intellectuals of Sierra Leone for the natives was widespread and the Sierra Leone workers were solid with the tribesmen. Should there be at any time a movement of the organized and educated blacks in the colony with a widespread peasant revolt in the protectorate, it would be difficult to prevent the Negroes of Sierra Leone and Gambia from gaining possession of the colony, though whether they would be able to keep it would depend upon events in other and wider spheres.

In Nigeria, a colony similar in social structure to Sierre Leone and Gambia, the crisis which began in 1929 produced the ex-

traordinary women's revolt in which over fifty women were killed
and over fifty wounded. The fall of prices for agrarian commodities placed the finances of the colony in difficulties, and the
Government attempted to recuperate its falling revenues by an
increase in direct taxation. Indirect rule works for the most part
through chiefs, many of whom are merely instruments of the
British Government. The chiefs were instructed to impose a tax
upon the women whereupon the slumbering discontent broke
out. Thousands of women organized protest demonstrations
against the Government and its chiefs and at Aba, the capital of
the Eastern Province, the women who sold in the market, faced
with the possibility of a tax which would destroy their small profits, organized a revolt. The writer is informed by Africans from
Nigeria that the actual happenings in Aba have been suppressed
in all official reports. The women seized public buildings and
held them for days. The servants refused to cook for their white
masters and mistresses and some of them made the attempt to
bring the European women by force into the markets to give them
some experience of what work was like. These saved themselves
only by precipitate flight, some of them with only the clothes
they had on their backs. A detachment of soldiers suppressed the
revolt, shooting at the black women as they tried to escape across
the river. Martial law was proclaimed and the Governor called
a meeting of the African editors in Lagos and threatened them
with imprisonment if they published news of what was happening at Aba. That is why written evidence is confined to the official
reports. A local committee of investigation was appointed and
issued a report which was approved by the Legislative Council.
Mr. Drummond Shiels, the labor Under-Secretary of State for the
Colonies, in answer to a question in the House of Commons replied that "the Colonial Office was satisfied that the officials on
the spot acted in the best interest of the country." But the publication of the report was the signal for a widespread agitation
throughout the colony. Mass meetings denounced it. The workers threatened to refuse to pay taxes; demanded a new commission, and redress of their economic and political grievances. The
Government was forced to appoint another commission. The
Negroes threatened to boycott it unless Africans were appointed

and the Government was forced to appoint two. This commission admitted economic grievances and suggested measures of reform. The Governor, however, imposed a fine of £850 on the town of Aba. Such was the resentment aroused that the political officers appealed to the Governor to withdraw the fine, and again the Governor had to capitulate.

The strength and vigor of the movement were a shock to the Europeans. Sir Frank Baddeley, the Colonial Secretary of Nigeria, found that the revolt was the work of the agents of Moscow. *The Times* Correspondent, however, gave a more sober estimate:

> The trouble was of a nature and extent unprecedented in Nigeria. In a country where the women throughout the centuries have remained in subjection to the men, this was eventually a women's movement, organized, developed and carried out by the women, without either the help or commission of their menfolk, though probably with their tacit sympathy.

Religious Revolts in New Colonies

The risings in Sierra Leone and Gambia are of a dual type. While the Negroes in the protectorates when driven to action think in terms of social revolution, those in the towns, like the majority of workers in Europe or America, aim at redress of immediate grievances, violent though their methods may be. Trade unions, the municipalities, the African press, have all given the movement its organized force, but of necessity make it more conservative.

In Eastern and Central Africa, more primitive territories, we have had during the last thirty years a series of risings of an entirely different type. In the years before the war, the tribes simply threw themselves at the government troops and suffered the inevitable defeat. Such risings could not go on. They were too obviously suicidal. In 1915, however, we have a new type—a rising led not by a tribal chief but by a Negro who has had some education. Such education as the African is given is nearly always religious, so that the leader often translated the insurrection into religious terms.

The Chilembwe rising in Nyasaland in 1915 was of this character. The first Europeans to arrive in Nyasaland were missionar-

ies sent out by the Church of Scotland. Soon after, many of them
left the mission for the land which they had acquired from the
native chiefs. They set up as coffee planters, converting the natives jointly to Christianity and to cheap labor. By 1915, these
plantations had passed into the hands of syndicates whose sole
object was to make the maximum profit. Within these plantations
which covered an area of 300 square miles and employed tens of
thousands of Negroes, the companies permitted no school, no
hospital and no missions.

A Negro, John Chilembwe by name, was sent to America by
a small mission nearby. After having had a good education, he
returned to his native land. He could find no position in any mission, so he built a church of his own with money raised from his
fellow blacks. Most of the white men in Africa hate Africans who
are educated and wear European clothes. His own treatment at
the hands of the white planters and missionaries and his readings
of the Bible, especially the story of the national struggle of the
Jews in the Old Testament, inspired Chilembwe to lead a revolt
against the European oppressors ("the Philistines").

Support for the revolt came mainly from the workers on
the estate and, according to plan, the five European heads of the
estate were killed. Their wives and children, however, met with
great kindness. The blacks spent money to get eggs and milk
for the white children, and banana leaves were held over their
heads to protect them from the sun on their journey away from
the estate.

The Europeans, frightened for their lives, ran to the military camps. But Chilembwe did not go very far. Just after he had
preached a sermon in the church, with the estate manager's head
on the pulpit, white police and soldiers appeared. The rebels took
to the jungle, but were rigorously hunted down. Among those
captured alive, about twenty were hanged, and all the rest sentenced to life terms. Chilembwe himself, old and nearly blind,
was shot down in the long grass with the other leaders.

Six years after, in 1921, the greatest of the religious type of re-
volt occurred in the Belgian Congo, and shook the whole colony.
The leader was Simon Kimbangu, a carpenter and a convert to
Christianity. In the spring of 1921 he had a dream in which he

was directed to go out and heal the sick. Kimbangu's influence immediately became very great among the native Christian converts. He appealed to the natives to leave the mission churches, controlled by their European masters, and to set up their own independent church organization under his guidance. To every African such a movement is an instinctive step toward independence and away from the perpetual control of Europeans. Negroes flocked in large numbers to Kimbangu, chiefly from the Protestant but from some of the Catholic missions as well. They declared they were tired of paying money to European churches.

The Government at first watched the movement uneasily but with tolerance. But the prophet's policy was soon seen to be detrimental to European interests in its implications. The natives left the plantations to listen to the Prophet, in much the same way as the Negro slaves in the West Indies a century before had been wont to plead religion and religious meetings as a convenient excuse for leaving the plantations at all times and without permission. The Negroes followed Kimbangu in such large numbers that industry was disorganized. Key plantations, upon which Government depended for the food for native employees in public utilities, were deserted. There was apprehension lest the natives should attempt to seize the lower Congo railway, which was indispensable to the colony. The fixing of Wednesday instead of Sunday as the day of rest created further dislocation. Worse still, as in all religious movements, minor "prophets" sprang up in the wake of the master, all professing to work miracles, but all more extreme than the Prophet himself. Their preachings tended to become more and more anti-European. Wealthy natives in Kinshasa gave the movement financial and ideological support. Native students from the British and French colonies joined the movement and spread radical doctrines among the rank and file. The movement became so threatening that in June 1921 the Belgian Government ordered Kimbangu's arrest.

Like a true prophet, Kimbangu escaped and this served only to strengthen his hold upon the masses. He stayed in one village and was visited by thousands of his followers, yet remained free until September, a striking testimony to his own influence and the strength and solidarity of his organization.

He was eventually tried by court-martial in October. It was held that Kimbangu's organization had aimed at overthrowing the Belgian regime, and that religion was only a means of inciting the population. Kimbangu was sentenced to death, his lieutenants to sentences of imprisonment varying from one year to life-time, while a girl, Mandobe, described as the most revolutionary woman in the Congo, received two years. The Negroes reacted with great violence. Strikes immediately broke out everywhere, to such an extent that European traders at Thysville petitioned the King that Kimbangu should be publicly hanged. The Africans threatened that Kimbangu's death would be followed by a general massacre of the whites and the Home Government commuted Kimbangu's sentence to life imprisonment and deported many of the minor leaders. The movement has been crushed but the natives continue to expect the reappearance of their "Messiah" and with it the departure of Europeans from the country.

We can conveniently deal here with the revolt of Africans in Kenya under the leadership of Harry Thuku. Harry Thuku, officially described as a man of base character, was very young, in his early twenties. He was a sort of petty clerk, and therefore had a little education, but he did not agitate in the name of God. He protested against high taxation, forced labor and other grievances. His propaganda touched even the smallest village and the state of an African colony is usually such that any strong leadership wins immediate support. The Thuku movement spread with great rapidity. It was estimated that at one meeting in Nairobi over 20,000 workers were enrolled.

Such a movement was too dangerous to be tolerated, and the Governor ordered mobilization of the native regiment, the King's African Rifles, to suppress it.

The Government supplemented force with trickery. It persuaded the chiefs to sign a proclamation appealing to the masses to return to work, and pledging the Government to reduce taxation and raise wages. This drove a wedge into Thuku's organization. The more timid accepted these promises, the movement subsided and Thuku was arrested. The arrest at once brought the masses out again, ready for a general strike. Crowds swarmed round Thuku's prison demanding his release. The soldiers were ordered to fire upon the crowd, and more than 150 were killed. The Negroes, however, were not intimidated. The Government circulated a rumor that Thuku would be transferred to another prison. This put the crowd on the wrong trail while Thuku was removed to a more remote and safer place. Hundreds were arrested, heavy fines were imposed, which in view of the low wages of the colony could only be liquidated by months of unremitting and unremunerative toil. All associations were declared illegal, and Thuku himself was shipped to Kismay on the Somali border, without trial.

The Congo

The Kimbangu movement took place in 1921. The Belgians, however, feared that there would be repetitions of the Kimbangu movement in a more extreme form. They were not mistaken. Indeed conditions in the Congo seem to produce an especially bitter and conscious type of revolt without any religious trimmings.

The difficulty here is to get accounts written in any detail. The British send out their punitive expeditions against revolting tribes and do not necessarily mention them in the annual colonial reports. But if the revolt awakens public interest, a commission will investigate and make a report. This report will frequently clash violently with the accounts of participants, eyewitnesses, correspondents of newspapers, native and European, and persons living in the colony at the time. The French and Belgians, however, publish little of this kind, and it is only indirectly that one can gain official confirmation of the vast revolts that have shaken the Belgian Congo since the days of Kimbangu. Thus, in the summer of 1932, M. Vandervelde, at one time Prime Minister of Belgium, spoke of the outrages in Belgian colonial administration and the revolts of the natives. In the course of his speech he said that lest he might make a mistake he had departed from his usual custom and was reading a part of his speech from notes. He told in detail the course of one revolt.

Three agents, sent to recruit workers in a Negro village, found only the women. The men, warned of their coming, had fled. The agents made the women kill cattle to feed them, then raped some of them. Some days after one of the Negroes, as is the custom in the Congo, demanded compensation. He was refused and lost his temper. He threw himself upon the white and bit him in the breast. This savage behavior gained him a severe flogging from his masters, who had him whipped until he bled, then handed in an indictment against him. An investigation began, but the natives fell on the official and cut him to pieces. Followed the inevitable punitive expedition to restore law and order and the damaged prestige of the whites. The officer in command found that the natives had fled into the bush. To continue with the expedition meant that they would remain there and many children would starve to death. The Governor was adamant. "We must," he telegraphed, "carry out an act of authority and defend the prestige of the Government before the population." The instruction was carried out. The natives fought back. They had only lances and other primitive weapons, but they fought for weeks. They died, says M. Vandervelde, in hundreds. But Lukutate, a native worker from Elizabethville, writing in the *Negro Worker* of July 1932, states that they died in thousands. Whole tribes, not knowing the effects of modern weapons, attacked the soldiers almost empty-handed. They starved in the forests. Some died under the whip, others were shot without trial in front of the women and children so as to warn them that blacks must never make rebellion against their white masters.

M. Vandervelde's account tallies very closely with that written by the Congo native. The files of the *Negro Worker* give many accounts of these revolts, and *The Life and Struggles of Negro Toilers*, by George Padmore, contains a great deal of coordinated information which is not easily obtainable elsewhere.

In 1924 there was a revolt in French Congo, lasting several days and suppressed by the French military authorities. In 1928, however, another revolt broke out, more class-conscious and better organized than the last. This lasted four months. The natives, despite the fewness of their arms, inflicted a number of defeats on the French troops, capturing a large section of the infantry. The fighting capacity of the revolutionaries, despite their handicaps, amazed even their enemies. The French shot all suspects, and whipped old men and women publicly in the villages as a warning. But by April 1930 the natives were rebelling again. A white French revolutionist and several natives were arrested at Brazzaville, capital of the Middle Congo, and sentenced to three years' imprisonment for attempting to organize a trade union. The natives, hearing of the sentence, went on strike and demonstrated before the court. The police attempted to break up the demonstration, but were attacked with stones. The soldiers were called out and without warning opened fire. The unequal fight continued until the natives were inevitably defeated. But the natives wounded the Governor of the Middle Congo, the troops had to occupy the native quarters of Brazzaville, and for days all business in the town was at a standstill.

This movement had definite Communist tendencies. What the authorities fear most is a combination of the workers in the towns and the peasants in the interior. Such a movement, however, has not yet taken place. The size of the territory, the differences of language, make such organization a task of great difficulty. Yet railways are linking the different portions of the territory, and in both French and Belgian Congo, French is becoming a *lingua franca* among those natives who get the chance to learn a little. Between 1921 and 1931 the whole temper of revolt in these territories has risen steadily. Since the war each succeeding revolt has been more fierce, more concentrated than the last.

Nor has the mandatory system made any essential difference. Rwanda-Urundi, formerly a part of German East Africa, is now mandated territory under the Belgian Government. Land alienation, or more precisely, taking away the natives' land, forced labor in the Katanga copper mines, all these typical features resulted in such a dislocation of local production, that the fields were not tilled and in 1929 a famine broke out in the district of Rwanda. Under the whip of hunger, the natives rose in revolt and the movement spread from Belgian Rwanda to British Uganda, where the tribes on the frontier also took up arms. The daughter of the King of Rwanda was one of the leaders of the revolutionaries, who made their first stroke at Gatsolon. There they killed a group of Belgian soldiers, officials, and native chiefs who were friendly with these whites. Belgian troops armed with modern weapons were brought to the scene, and against them the natives, armed only with spears and knives, battled for weeks. The masses of natives fled from the double scourge of famine and machine-guns. Where they fell, some of the bodies, still living, were devoured by wild animals. As was inevitable, the revolt was beaten down. The leaders fled through the swamps until they reached the Uganda frontier. There the British arrested them and handed them over to the Belgians. Over 1,000 tribesmen were shot and a Belgian regiment and a British detachment of the East African Rifles were stationed in Kiforte, the center of the revolt.

The difference between the native under Belgian imperialism plain and simple, and Belgian imperialism carrying out the mandate of the League of Nations, is that the Belgian Government presents a report at Geneva on the working of the mandate. The native, however, is not likely to know this.

The Union of South Africa

The post-war period in South Africa has given us at least two clearly-marked types of Negro revolutionary activity, the Bondelzwarts revolt and the Industrial and Commercial Workers' Union. The Bondelzwarts revolt belongs in spirit to the early tribal revolts, that of the tribes beating their heads against a wall.

The Bondelzwarts are a tribe of Hottentots inhabiting the extreme southern portion of South-West Africa. They have actually never been fully conquered by Europeans, and their history is full of struggles against the Germans. After their last rebellion against the German Government, the leaders of the tribe, Jacobus Christian and Abraham Morris, were compelled to leave the territory and reside in the Cape Province. When the Germans were defeated during the war, Jacobus Christian asked the new authorities for permission to enter. He was refused. But in 1919, disregarding the Government's order, he returned to his native country. In April 1922, Abraham Morris, the other exiled leader, also returned home with a group of followers. On entering the territory he handed over his gun to the police, as required by the law. But the magistrate was not satisfied with that, and considering him a dangerous character, sent the police to arrest him and five of his followers. Morris resisted the arrest, and the people threatened to use violence on his behalf. When called upon to assist the police, all headmen refused, and the people working on the neighboring farms abandoned their work and began to assemble at Haib, the headquarters of Jacobus Christian.

On May 12, Major van Coller with a police force was sent to effect the arrest of the "five criminals." He sent a message to Jacobus Christian to come and see him at Dreihoek, but, seeing the trap, Christian refused. The discontent of the people suddenly crystallized around their leader's arrest. Patrols of armed Hottentots forcibly collected arms from isolated European farmers, and at one farm, as the Administration later stated, "European women were forced to prepare and pour out coffee for the Hottentots."

On May 16, Jacobus Christian sent a statement to the Administrator stating that the five men would immediately report to the magistrate on condition that he received an assurance, in writing, from the Administrator, that no further steps would be taken against his people. This the Administrator refused to do, and both sides prepared for an armed struggle. Haib, the headquarters of the Bondelzwarts, was placed under martial law by Jacobus Christian. Armed pickets guarded all the roads and passers-by were subjected to the scrutiny of these guards. When Major van Coller, being unable to make Christian come to Dreihoek, was compelled to go to see him at Haib, he, a Major of the South-West African police, was stopped by armed pickets who allowed him to go to see the leader only after close examination. In his report he afterward stated that the Bondelzwarts were all assembled and "judging from their dispositions they are prepared to meet an armed force. They gave attentive hearing and showed no hostility toward us, but there was visible demurrance when they were told that arms and ammunition were to be surrendered."

The struggle broke out on May 26, 1922. The forces of the rebels were very poor. The tribe had only six hundred men capable of bearing arms, and these six hundred had only about one hundred rifles. Against this ill-armed force, the South African Government sent 445 well-armed men, equipped with artillery, machine-guns, mechanical transport, and two airplanes. Yet the fighting lasted for nearly two weeks. The Bondelzwarts at first evaded big battles and tried to elude the Government forces. But they were surrounded and one big battle was fought in the mountains. Only the use of airplanes, something new and un-expected to the black warriors, compelled them to surrender. The number of killed will probably never be known. This was essentially a tribal revolt of the old prewar type. But the resist-ance reached a pitch of calm determination to fight and die rather than give in, which makes it one of the most significant of African risings.

The Bondelzwarts revolt was an anachronism in 1922. The Union of South Africa is marked by a new type of political ac-tion—not the instinctive revolt of primitive tribes, but the mili-tant action of the proletariat in the towns. Far more than in Sierra Leone and Gambia, South African industry has brought the natives together in factories, mines and on the docks, and the circumstances of their employment tended to drive them toward industrial organization in the modern manner. There is also the influence of the Russian Revolution. The South African Communist Party was founded only in 1924, but it had its ori-gin in a previous organization which was already in existence in 1920. It directed its propaganda chiefly to the natives. But whereas in Sierra Leone and Gambia the Negro intelligentsia of the Left for the moment are more vocal than effective, the South African system allows very few of these to exist and drives even the few that are there into militant opposition. From these post-war conditions and the economic and political crisis of 1919 sprang the Industrial and Commercial Workers' Union of South Africa.

It was formed in 1919 by a Nyasaland native, Clements Kadalie, and the organization began with only twenty-four members. Without any help in finance, experience or encour-agement, suffering persecution and arrest, these built a move-ment which matured in strikes, demonstrations and battles with the police, while white South Africa watched its incredible growth with alarm. Kadalie, as a native of Nyasaland, could eas-ily have been deported, but somehow he escaped this fate and drove his movement forward.

The first sign of the I.C.U.'s real strength was the Port Elizabeth strike of 1920. The Port Elizabeth workers, mainly unskilled laborers, had demanded and obtained an increase of sixpence a day. In February 1920, a branch of the I.C.U. was formed in Port Elizabeth. This demanded a further increase of sixpence a day and as a consequence of fresh agitation, the workers obtained it. But this did not satisfy them and, on the advice of Kadalie, the President of the I.C.U., they advanced a demand for a minimum daily wage of ten shillings for unskilled male workers and seven shillings and sixpence for adult females. Meetings were held all over the district by the I.C.U., at which workers were called upon to insist on this demand even to the point of a strike. This I.C.U. agitation had a tremendous effect. Feeling was running high and the influence of Kadalie was increasing. At one meeting, the feelings of the workers were so aroused that some made a physical attack on Dr. Rubusama, also a Negro, who was known to be opposed to Kadalie. Dr. Rubusama was only rescued by Kadalie who, on seeing his danger, immediately intervened.

The police, in the meanwhile, were looking for an excuse to arrest Kadalie. This attack on Dr. Rubusama was used as a pretext. Rubusama made an affidavit concerning the attack on him, and Kadalie was arrested on October 23, 1920, without a warrant.

When news of the arrest became known, the workers congregated in the nearest square. A meeting was held and a deputation was sent to the police to ask for the release of Kadalie on bail. The chief of police refused. When the deputation returned with this news the meeting resolved to send an ultimatum to the police: unless Kadalie was released by five o'clock, they would release him themselves. The South African native was openly challenging not only white employers but the actual forces of the state.

The whole police force was armed. The railway police were called out. In addition, European volunteers were armed and stationed in front of the police station where Kadalie was detained. By five o'clock the demonstration numbered 3,000 people.

The mounted police were ordered to charge, but they were unhorsed. An attempt was made to disperse the crowd by means of a water-hose. But the masses replied with stones and other missiles. At this stage two shots were fired and the crowd began to retreat. It was at this moment, while the crowd was running, that the police opened fire upon it. The official Commission of Inquiry stated:

> It is established beyond doubt that immediately af-
> ter the first shots were fired, the crowd stampeded
> in all directions, and that a rapid and sustained fu-
> sillade was directed on the retreating crowd from the
> police station for sixty seconds, as alleged by some
> witnesses, or two minutes as alleged by others. One
> civilian admitted firing fifteen shots; another as many
> as thirteen shots, with the most fatal results, viz.: one
> European and twenty-three natives or colored males
> were killed or died of wounds. Native and colored
> males wounded, forty-five; females, one. European
> females wounded, four. Total casualties, seventy-six.
> Only two of these were shot immediately in front of
> the steps, the others fell in different parts of the street
> away from the police station, as far as Castle Street,
> 100 yards distant.

Obviously the police were seizing the opportunity to smash the workers' organization once and for all. The net result, as so often, was to increase its strength.

So powerful a force did the I.C.U. become among the Bantu and colored people that Hertzog, a future Prime Minister of South Africa, thought it profitable to seek the support of the I.C.U. in the Cape Province. He sent a very cordial letter to Kadalie, enclosing a donation to the I.C.U., saying that he was sorry that he could not do more.

Of course, immediately Hertzog gained power, he persecuted the I.C.U. even more fiercely. But the movement continued to grow, and in 1926 it reached its peak. In that year it had a membership of 100,000. Teachers were leaving the profession to become agents of the I.C.U. In remote villages of South Africa one could find a representative. Many who had not joined rallied to it in time of difficulty.

It will be difficult to over-estimate what Kadalie and his partner, Champion, achieved between 1919 and 1926. Kadalie was an orator, tall, with a splendid voice, and at his meetings he used to arouse the Bantu workers to great heights of enthusiasm. At the conclusion of the speech his hearers were usually silent for some seconds before they were able to begin the applause. Champion was the very opposite of Kadalie in everything. More backward in outlook than Kadalie, who was aware of the working-class movement as an international force, he saw very little beyond Zululand, or Natal, and he was more organizer than orator.

The real parallel to this movement is the mass uprising in San Domingo. There is the same instinctive capacity for organization, the same throwing-up of gifted leaders from among the masses. But whereas there was a French Revolution in 1794 rooting out the old order in France, needing the black revolution, and sending out encouragement, organizers and arms, there was nothing like that in Britain. Seen in that historical perspective, the Kadalie movement can be understood for the profoundly important thing it was.

After 1926 the movement began to decline. It could not maintain itself for long at that pitch without great and concrete successes. It was bound to stabilize itself at a less intense level. Kadalie lacked the education and the knowledge to organize it on a stable basis—the hardest of all tasks for a man of his origin. There was misappropriation of the funds. He saw the necessity for international affiliation. But though the constitution of the organization condemned capitalism, he would not affiliate to the Third International. The white South African workers refused his offer of unity, for these, petit-bourgeois in outlook owing to their high wages and the social degradation of the Negro, are among the bitterest enemies of the native workers. Kadalie came to Europe, affiliated the I.C.U. to the International Federation of Trade Unions and sought the help of left-wing labor members. He took back a white man, Ballinger, to assist him. But the decline of the I.C.U. continued. The organization split. Today the two sections are but a shadow of the early I.C.U., and Kadalie keeps a cafe, in Port Elizabeth, where formerly the workers had been shot down while demonstrating for his release.

5

Marcus Garvey

During the very period, 1919–1926, that the natives in South Africa were organizing themselves, a similar movement was taking place among the Negroes in America. A large population, more literacy, the greater wealth of the Negro and greater facilities for publicity and communication, made this movement the biggest Negro organization yet known. It is known as the Garvey Movement.

To understand the Garvey Movement one must have some idea of the status of the Negro even in modern America. The period of "reconstruction" did not last long and the Southern whites soon re-established their old domination on the new basis of Negro freedom. In many areas they prevented the Negro from voting, either by inventing fantastic qualifications such as those which find a Negro graduate of Harvard or Yale unable to exercise the franchise through lack of education; or quite simply by parading armed men before the polling booth and warning the Negro what would happen to him if he attempted to come near. In states such as Texas, the Negro is made to feel his color at every turn. He cannot ride in the Pullman cars, he must sit at the back of the streetcars; in certain areas he can own only a Ford car; the white always has the right of way in the street. The Negro must make up his mind that his black skin makes him a servant and he must remain so. Periodically, some years at the rate of more than one a week, a Negro is lynched by a howling mob of white citizens. In the more liberal North there is race prejudice, though it is not nearly so acute.

Both in North and South, certain Negroes have emerged as businessmen, professional men, artists, writers, musicians. Some of them do astonishingly well and the circle of Negro intelligentsia is daily increasing. Yet the prevailing attitude to the Negro is one of strong and sometimes ferocious prejudice.

Before the Negro can struggle intelligently against this, in order that the layman may appreciate the efforts which have been made and the possibilities of success, it is necessary to inquire more closely as to the origin of this powerful prejudice which inevitably awakens kindred feelings in the Negroes. There is no question here as in Africa of alien civilizations. The American Negro, in language, tradition and culture is an American. He was in America almost from the beginning and he has helped to make the country what it is. Hostility to him on the part of the whites is not a question of physiological repugnance. The numerous half-breeds, the unceasing miscegenation in America as well as in so strong a fortress of race prejudice as South Africa, prove this. That the color bar exists only in daylight is a proverb common in Africa as well as in America. A Southern white woman will be nursed by a Negro wet-nurse, and will pass her childhood days with Negro servants. As she grows up she will be taught to ride by a black groom. Black servants will cook her food and wait on her at table. A young Southern woman, it is common knowledge, often has far more confidence in her old black nurse than in her own relations. A black chauffeur will drive her into town. She enters a restaurant, sees a Negro sitting 40 feet away having a meal, and shrieks that he must be put out. Obviously she feels no physical repugnance. This is a social and political question. The Negro must be kept in his place. This is the main reason for the Southern persecution of the Negro. As worker, as tenant-farmer, as sharecropper, he is at the mercy of his employer and he must be terrorized into acceptance of whatever conditions of life are offered to him.

What are the reasons usually offered for the attitude of the Southern whites toward Negroes? Sex is the one most usually urged: the Negro cannot subdue his passion for white women. Yet of 130 Negro revolts that took place between 1670 and 1865 in America, there is not a single case recorded of a white woman being raped by the revolting slaves. In the West Indies, since the abolition of slavery, there has not been one single case of rape or sexual assault by a Negro against a white woman. While the thousands of cases of Negroes lynched in America during the last half-century, charges of rape have been made in only twenty percent of cases. With what justification some of these charges have been made the Scottsboro case has within recent years given a glaring example. It is not strange that this is so. Sir Harry Johnston after his vast experience of Africa shows on what ground similar agitation has been raised against African Negroes:

> There is, I am convinced, a deliberate tendency in the Southern States to exaggerate the desire of the Negro for a sexual union with white women and the crimes he may commit under this impulse. A few exceptional Negroes in West and South Africa, and in America, are attracted towards a white consort, but almost invariably for honest and pure-minded reasons, because of some intellectual affinity or sympathy. The mass of the race, if left free to choose, would prefer to mate with women of its own type. "When cases have occurred in the history of South Africa, South-West, East and Central Africa, of some great Negro uprising, and the wives and daughters of officials, missionaries and settlers have been temporarily at the mercy of a Negro

army, or in the power of a Negro chief, how extremely
rare are the proved cases of any sexual abuse arising
from this circumstance! How infinitely rarer than
the prostitution of Negro women following on some
great conquest of their whites or of their black or yel-
low allies! I know that the contrary has been freely al-
leged and falsely stated in histories of African events;
but when the facts have been really investigated, it is
little else than astonishing that the Negro has either
had too great a racial sense of decency, or too little lik-
ing for the white women (I believe it to be the former
rather than the latter) to outrage the unhappy white
women and girls temporarily in his power. He may
have dashed out the brains of the white babies against
a stone, have even killed, possibly, their mothers, or
taken them and the unmarried girls as hostages into
the harem of a chief (where no attempt has ever been
made upon their virtue), but in the history of the various Kaffir wars it is remarkable how in the majority of
cases the wives and daughters of the British, the Boers,
and the Germans, after the slaughter of their male relations, were sent back unharmed to white territory.

All Negroes are aware of the mass of lies on which the prejudice is built, of the propaganda which is designed to cover the naked economic exploitation. But the Negro and his white friends
have little chance to stem the propaganda. The main organs of
publicity are in the hands of the whites. The millions who watch
the films always see Negroes shining shoes or doing menial work,
singing or dancing. Of the thousands of Negro professional men,
of the nearly two hundred Negro universities and colleges in
America which give degrees in every branch of learning, and are
run predominantly by Negro professors—of this the American
capitalist takes good care that nothing appears on the screen.

Thus the American Negro—literate, Westernized, an
American almost from the foundation of America—suffers from
his humiliations and discriminations to a degree that few whites
and even many non-American Negroes can ever understand. The
jazz gaiety of the American Negro is a semi-conscious reaction

to the fundamental sorrow of the race. Often lynching is not the spontaneous madness of a crowd, but a demonstration carefully organized and announced in the press as being fixed for the next day. The American whites will burn a Negro alive. Less than ten years ago a crowd of white men, women and children danced round a burning Negro singing "Happy days are here again." Little by little the Negro in the South, particularly in the towns, is fighting his way to better conditions. But the continuity of white policy is unbroken from 1650 to 1930. The Negro must be kept down. That is the background of Negro American life.

During the [1914–1918] war thousands of Negroes emigrated from the South to the North where there was work to be had, high pay, and racial discrimination was less offensive. Negro soldiers fought in the war and suffered not only from the race prejudice of their own officers, but, welcomed by the French, saw the American whites, by word and deed and written memoranda, seek to poison the French against them. So fiercely did the white Americans attack them that the French asked to take them over. The black regiment was brigaded with a French division and fought as a French unit. The first American to win the *Croix-de-Guerre* was a Negro. The regiment fought with great gallantry and when the war was over the French General Staff, appreciative and courteous according to their lights, gave these visitors the honor of being the first allied regiment to march into German territory. This did not make the blacks love the Americans any better. They came home bitter and disillusioned, to find that they had shed their blood in the war for democracy and faced the same undemocratic conditions as before.

In August 1914, Marcus Garvey, a Jamaican Negro, a printer, and Amy Ashwood, his friend, almost a schoolgirl, founded the Universal Negro Improvement Association in Kingston, Jamaica. They were the only members, and she appointed him the President, and he appointed her the Secretary. They carried on propaganda in Jamaica for two years, and then Garvey went to the United States, the Mecca of all West Indian Negroes before the slump. Amy Ashwood went to New York to meet him in 1918, and the U.N.I.A. then had seventeen members. Garvey spoke and agitated, and by 1919 he had about 5,000 members attached to his organization. Then he got arrested for libeling the Assistant District Attorney of New York. Negroes all over America were suddenly aware of him. The soldiers were coming back home, bringing their bitterness and their money. There was a boom and Negroes shared in it. Revolution was in the air, and the Negroes were ready for revolution.

There has never been a Negro movement anywhere like the Garvey Movement, and few movements in any country can be compared to it in growth and intensity. By 1920 it was proportionately the most powerful mass movement in America. Supporters of Garvey have claimed that the U.N.I.A. membership in 1920 reached three million, and Garvey himself claimed in 1924 six million. The latter figure is certainly exaggerated, for that would have meant at least half of the total Negro population of America at that time. That nine-tenths of the Negroes in America were listening to him is probable, and as far as can be gathered, from very insufficient data, he may well have had two million members already in 1920. Money and members poured in from every state in America, from all over the West Indies, from Panama. Negroes sold their dearest possessions to send money to Garvey. His name rolled through Africa. The King of Swaziland told a friend some years after that he knew the names of only two black men in the Western world: Jack Johnson and Marcus Garvey.

What was Garvey's program? Back to Africa. The Negroes must have Africa back for themselves. They would go and settle there and live in Africa as free and happy as Europeans lived in Europe and white Americans in America. How were they to get Africa back? They would ask the imperialists for it, and if the imperialists did not give it, they would take it back. That was in essence all that Garvey had to say. True, he attacked lynching, he formulated militant demands, equal rights for Negroes, democratic liberties, etc. But the program was essentially: Back to Africa.

It was pitiable rubbish, but the Negroes wanted a leader and they took the first that was offered them. Furthermore, desperate men often hear, not the actual words of an orator but their own thoughts. Daniel O'Connell preached the Repeal of the Union [in Britain], but the large majority of Irish peasants thought in terms of the expulsion of the British and the seizure of the land. And Garvey was a man of exceptional gifts. He was an orator, at his best a very great orator indeed, opportunist to the bone, skillful in tuning his words to his audience. But his words were always militant, and the Negroes listened, paid their money and waited. All the things that Hitler was to do so well later Garvey was doing in 1920 and 1921. He organized stormtroopers, who marched, uniformed, in his parades, and kept order and gave color to his meetings. He understood what was then supposed to be the psychology of the Negro with his childlike mentality. (But this was before some of the greatest peoples in Europe were swept off their feet by the same antics and promiscuous promises.) And while Garvey whipped up his audiences, like Hitler, he organized his millions of adherents with a German thoroughness.

It is not improbable that the strength of the movement he had unloosed took Garvey by surprise. He and his wife covered the country, enrolling members. He built a hall, Liberty Hall, he organized mass demonstrations and congresses. He appointed himself President, Emperor, King and what not, of Africa, and created a string of Negro nobility, and titled followers, from Dukes to plain baronets. He sent deputations to the League of Nations asking for Africa. He embarked on a steamship scheme, the Black Star Line, and actually bought one or two ships that actually made one or two voyages. "The Black Star Line will sail to Africa if it sails in seas of blood." But program for the Afro-Americans he had none, not even a bad one.

Despite his militancy, furthermore, Garvey was confused. He attacked imperialism, but he was ready to propound the doctrine that the Negro must be loyal to all flags under which he lives. He viciously attacked Communism and advised the Negro workers against linking up with white workers in industrial struggles. He negotiated with the Ku Klux Klan for the repatriation of Negroes to Liberia. From about 1921 it was already clear that his aims were beyond achievement. But he was a man of great physical courage, he continued to hold great meetings, some of them in Madison Square, with police constantly striving to arrest him, and sometimes succeeding. He indulged in some unsound business schemes. He sent agents to Liberia, but the Liberian Government, satellites of America, would have little to do with them, and it is doubtful if Garvey ever intended to do anything serious. Yet for years he continued to have a huge mass following and exercised a powerful influence on millions of Negroes in America and all over the world. In 1926 he was charged for using the United States mail with intent to defraud. He was convicted, imprisoned, and then deported to Jamaica. There he at once began an evolution the signs of which had long been evident. He quickly made his peace with British imperialism. His movement disintegrated.

One thing Garvey did do. He made the American Negro conscious of his African origin and created for the first time a feeling of international solidarity among Africans and people of African descent. In so far as this is directed against oppression it is a progressive step. But his movement was in many respects absurd and in others thoroughly dishonest. It has resulted in a widespread disillusionment. Unlike Kadalie, he was *petit bourgeois* in origin and never thought in terms of industrial organization. Yet the Garvey Movement like the I.C.U. in its best days, though it actually achieved little in proportion to its size, is of immense importance in the history of Negro revolts. It shows the fires that smolder in the Negro world, in America as in Africa.

6

Negro Movements in Recent Years

In the British Empire, there have been a series of Negro movements since the Ottawa
Conference in 1932. This drove cheap
Japanese goods out of the colonies and
brought in British just at the time when the
blacks were impoverished by the world crisis.
The ensuing response to subversive propaganda led to the passing of drastic sedition
bills. Thus the colonies have been, in recent
years, the scene of revolt after revolt in the
West Indies, in West Africa, in East Africa,
and Mauritius. Let us take some of these
revolts and try to analyze their particular
significance.

The Gold Coast, one of the old colonies, has recently experienced an upheaval.
In 1937, in the Gold Coast and in Ashanti,

a district in the interior, the cocoa farmers organized themselves against the "Pool" set up by the commercial firms and made up their minds to smash it. Early in 1938 the motor drivers, protesting against heavy fines for trivial offenses (imposed by an African magistrate) struck, and brought motor traffic to a standstill. The boat-boys went on strike. The strike was general, and a boycott of European merchandise was proclaimed. Anyone found buying or selling European imported goods was assaulted, carried before a chief and penalized. Sir Ofori Atta, a typical Government chief, supported the strike, so strong was the pressure of the masses. The population of Cape Coast, a seaport town in the Gold Coast, staged a mass demonstration against a new water-rate. The police tried to interfere and were driven back to the station, which was razed to the ground. The Government ordered police and soldiers to Cape Coast. Their way lay through Saltpond. The people of Saltpond barricaded the road and resisted the soldiers and police, who were driven back. By the time they reached Cape Coast all was calm.

An extraordinary determination and unity linked the population. An unconfirmed report stated that, being owners of their land, the Cape Coast people gave notice to the United Africa Company, Lord Leverhulme's combine, to quit, this by way of protest against the water-rate. At the expiration of the notice they forced the stores open and put the goods outside. Owing to the motor strike there were no lorries to take these away, and they were looted.

Militant as was this movement, yet, as in most of the older colonies, there was not that militancy which thinks in terms of throwing out the British. The West Africans are increasingly proud, nationalistic, jealous of discrimination, but there is no national revolutionary movement. A Cocoa Commission from Britain helped to restore quiet and is preparing a report.

In the West Indian colony of Trinidad there has been an even more powerful movement.

The victory of the San Domingo blacks gave the final blow to the slave trade in the West Indies. Britain abolished the trade in 1807 and slavery itself was abolished in 1834, due to the economic decline of the West Indies, the vigorous attacks of the abolitionists, and the support of the new industrial bourgeoisie to whom the privileges of the West Indies sugar planters were detrimental. The great insurrection in Jamaica in 1831 contributed materially to hasten the process. The Negroes in the West Indian islands have therefore developed in a manner peculiar to themselves. The blacks speak French, English or Spanish. They have lost all sense of their African origin and have become Westernized in their outlook. A Negro and Mulatto middle class has emerged. Racial prejudice and discrimination, though by no means abolished, have gradually declined. Though the whites control most of the industries, the Negro middle classes are gradually monopolizing the professions and the civil service. The Negroes are not a minority as in America, are trained in the Western manner, and the whites therefore cannot take undue liberties with them.

Socially the situation is in no way comparable to that in Central or Southern Africa or the Southern States. In Trinidad a few years ago a white South African was appointed to a post in the civil service. For some reason or other he kicked a black laborer who immediately kicked him back. The South African was charged. The magistrate on the bench, a colored man, fined him. He was made to understand that he was no longer in South Africa, and that if he did not mend his ways, he would be sent to prison. Most of the colonies are governed by the Colonial Office, and driven by the confused, but steady pressure of the masses for improvement, the Colonial Office evades the issue by appointing more and more men of color to the higher posts in the service. The islands produce colored men of great intellectual brilliance who have distinguished careers in the inns of court, the hospitals and in the British universities. The colored middle classes are making great progress. They grumble at racial discrimination, but their outlook is the same as that of the rich whites, and indeed their sole grievances are that they do not get all the posts they want, and that the whites do not often invite them to dinner.

The real difficulty of the West Indies is the poverty of the masses. The islands have been steadily declining in economic importance. The black and Mulatto intelligentsia sometimes use radical phases, but for the most part are interested solely in their own advancement. The Henry Norman Commission at the end of the last century recommended the break-up of the large estates and the spread of peasant proprietorship, but the officials and the nominated members of the Legislative Councils do not concern themselves with such projects, and malnutrition, bad housing conditions and low wages seemed to be the permanent fate of the Negro masses. The 1929 crisis and Ottawa have increased the burden on the poor. This situation has resulted in growing radicalization of the masses, a sharpening of racial feeling and a growing social and political tension in the islands. It reached its climax in Trinidad last year [1937], and that the movement assumed the proportions that it did in Trinidad is no accident, and shows how human nature responds to environment, in London, China and Peru.

Trinidad has a population of some four hundred thousand people, of whom over one-third are Indians, the descendants of men and women brought to the island from India as indentured laborers. Between them and the blacks there is no racial ill-feeling. As in South Africa and America, 1919 was a period of great unrest in the West Indies. There was a general strike of the dockers. They patrolled the town, made business close down, and were at one time in charge of the city. The white industrialists clamored that cruisers should be sent for and the mere landing of armed sailors was sufficient to restore the *status quo*. There was little organized industry, and as in Barbados, even up to the present day, artisans and unskilled laborers find it difficult to organize themselves. The writer was in the island at that time, and one feature of the disturbances caused widespread comment in informed circles: while the workers were in control of the town, the police were singularly inactive. It was stated that the officer in command was subjected to an inquiry and made good his contention that he could not trust his black policemen to shoot at the black workers. Race feeling is not acute at normal times. Children of all colors are educated together at the secondary schools. Whites, blacks, browns, Indians and Chinese play cricket and football together on afternoons, sometimes in the same team, and the various members of the community turn out to cheer their respective sides. West Indian cricket teams composed of all colors tour England and Australia together without undue friction and with a great deal of friendliness in many cases. But the division of rich and poor is also the division of white and black, and in moments of tension can become very acute. For the same reason, however, the possibility is greater here than elsewhere, that the police might take sides with the workers, and that is an ever present difficulty which is to be solved by the cruiser—as long as cruisers are available.

Between 1919 and 1937 Trinidad, like the other West Indian islands, has lived an increasingly active political life. Self-government is one of the questions of the day, and the Legislative Council now has elected members. What has created the new Trinidad, however, has been the development of the oil indus-try, which now employs nearly 10,000 men concentrated in the southern part of the island. Large-scale industry has had the in-evitable result of developing a high sense of labor solidarity and growing political consciousness. The slump threw the population into great poverty and the inadequacy of the social services in-tensified the resultant suffering. The Ethiopian question sharp-ened the sense of racial solidarity and racial oppression. News of the stay-in [sit down] strikes in France and America was eagerly read by these workers. They found a leader in Uriah Butler, an agitator with a religious bias.

Butler's career, despite his religion, is identical with that of many revolutionaries in Western Europe. Since the war the leader of the workers' movement in Trinidad has been Captain Cipriani, a white man who identified himself with the interests of the black masses and did very fine work on their behalf. His Labor Party is a loose political organization, which protected the industrial interests of the workers as far as it could, agitated for self-govern-ment and was for years the only mass political organization in the island. But Cipriani is a reformist. Butler was a member of this party, he wanted militant industrial action and was expelled for holding "Communistic" views and being "extremist." He went to the South and carried on his agitation among the oilfield work-ers. In June of last year the oilfield workers staged a stay-in strike for higher wages. The consequences were unprecedented.

The Government tried to arrest Butler while he was address-ing a crowd. The crowd resisted the arrest and the police had to retire. One Corporal King, a Negro (notorious in the district for his hostility to the workers), followed Butler. He was set upon by the crowd, and in attempting to escape, fell and broke his leg. While he lay on the ground he was beaten, oil was poured upon him and he was burned to death. The episode is almost identical with the lynchings of Negroes in the Southern states. King was a black man, but his whole career had identified him with the whites, and reports from the island state that the regrets expressed are not for the burning but that it was not one of "them"—meaning the whites. Later in the day the police were fired upon and a sub-inspector was killed.

Thenceforth the strike spread. Destruction of property may have been the work of certain hooligan elements, as the official report states, but the strike was complete in Port-of-Spain, the capital, a town of 80,000 inhabitants, which is at the opposite end of the island, some 40 miles away from the scene of the first outbreak. This, the most outstanding feature of the disturbances, is referred to parenthetically in the official report as follows: "The same morning Port-of-Spain, where work at all the industrial establishments had ceased." The Indian agricultural laborers, who might appear to have little in common with the black proletariat, no sooner saw these blacks in militant action than they too followed them and began to strike. In many parts of the island stoppage of work was complete. The Government sent for one cruiser. But whereas in 1919 the unrest subsided at the appearance of the sailors, much has happened since then, and the people were quite unmoved at the appearance of the first, and even of a second, cruiser. The Governor had taken a strong line at first, but, in the face of the determination of the population, he and one of the leading officials used language hostile to the white employers and attempted conciliation. The Governor has been censured for this and has now retired from the colonial service. His action was probably justified.

Though the Commission's report denies it, information from the spot states that race feeling was rampant, and it needed little to precipitate a general attack on the whites. It could hardly have been otherwise, for the Governor himself stressed the importance of the Ethiopian question in sharpening the political tension in the island. The majority of Negroes everywhere have the misguided belief that the blacks of Ethiopia were betrayed by the whites because they were black. The Commission has admitted the grievous condition of the poor in the island, and have thus indirectly justified the strike. What is important, however, is the political awakening which it has crystallized. The Commission's report merely hints at, but does not state that, the workers demanded the forty-hour week, holidays with pay, and it is stated, though this is not as yet certain, a share of the profits. They demanded equal pay with white men for the same work, they showed their resentment against South African whites who have attempted to treat them in a way to which they have not been accustomed. After returning to work they again went on strike to force recognition of their newly formed union. Captain Cipriani, their idol for years, was not in the island at the time of the strike and spoke against them. They threw him and his party over at once. Trade unions are being formed all over the island, and the advanced workers are clamoring for revolutionary literature of all sorts, by Marx and Engels and other writers on Communism, and literature dealing with the Ethiopian question. In the recent elections, in the key Southern constituency, the workers' candidate was Mr. Rienzi, an Indian lawyer, president of the new unions. Some of his opponents tried to raise the race question, Negro as opposed to Indian. But Rienzi had fought with them side by side all through the days of the strike. They refused to be distracted. They and their leaders poured scorn on the racial question and proclaimed that the issue was one of class. Thus these workers have almost at a single bound placed themselves in the forefront of the international working class movement. The Government is now seeking to pass a drastic bill imposing heavy penalties for the mere possession of radical far less revolutionary literature. The white employers are calling for soldiers to be stationed in the island. It is certain that racial feeling will gradually take a less prominent part in the struggle than hitherto, for the Negro middle classes are already aligning themselves and making the issue clear. They are with the whites. Industrialization has been the decisive factor here. While it is unwise to predict, the clamor for literature shows how strong is the urge to know what is happening abroad and follow suit. Already a local pamphlet has been written on Fascism. The movement is clearly on its way to a link with the most advanced workers in Western Europe. This is a stage far beyond the Gold Coast. This study was already in proof when the Jamaica revolt forced the appointment of a Royal Commission. The Negroes in British Guiana are also simmering with unrest. In Trinidad mass demonstrations are still taking place. The history of all these territories is in essence the history of Trinidad. Consideration of the remedies is beyond us but they will need to be far-reaching.

The third and last of the recent revolts selected for treatment here took place as far back as 1935. Yet it is of more importance than the other two. Trinidad is but a small island in the West Indies, the coastal districts of West Africa are but a fringe to the millions of Negroes in Central, East and Southern Africa. The report of the Commission of Inquiry on the revolt of the Rhodesian miners in 1935 gives a very clear picture of what is going on in the mind of the great masses of Africans.

Northern Rhodesia is a new type of colony. It is like Kenya in that there is no sort of buffer class in between the white settlers and the Negroes. There is, however, an industrial proletariat in the copper mines, and this at once gives native resentment weight. The wages are round about fifteen shillings a month, with the usual complement of segregation and racial discrimination. In October 1935, there was a strike in the mines. The tax had been abruptly raised and the workers protested in the only way they could. Soldiers were rushed to the spot, six natives were killed and twenty-two wounded, and peace restored. From all appearances this is hardly a revolt, but merely a strike which has got out of hand. Such a view would completely misunderstand the present situation in Africa and be wholly false. This, for instance, is a native translation of the call for the strike.

> Listen to this all you who live in the country, think well how they treat us and to ask for a land. Do we live in good treatment, no; therefore let us ask one another and remember this treatment. Because we wish on the day of 29th April, every person not to go to work, he who will go to work, and if we see him it

will be a serious case. Know how they cause us to suffer, they cheat us for money, they arrest us for loafing,
they persecute us and put us in gaol for tax. What reason have we done? Secondly do you not wish to hear
these words, well listen, this year of 1935, if they will
not increase us more money stop paying tax, do you
think they can kill you, no. Let us encourage surely
you will see that God will be with us. See how we suffer with the work and how we are continually reviled
and beaten underground. Many brothers of us die for
22s. 6d., is this money that we should lose our lives
for. He who cannot read should tell his companion
that on the 29th April not to go to work. These words
do not come from here, they come from the wisers
who are far away and enable to encourage us.

> That all. Hear well if it is right let us do so.
> We are all of the Nkana
> Africans—Men and Women.
> I am glad,
> G. LOVEWEY

It is clear that this is no mere appeal to strike but a summons
to relentless struggle with mortal enemies. Should world events
give these people a chance, they will destroy what has them by the
throat as surely as the San Domingo blacks destroyed the French
plantocracy. This note of having endured to the limit and being
ready to resist to the death occurs in another notice found by
accident which states: "Nobody must go to work on the 1st May.
All tribes and people. We shall die. They will kill us on Friday.
P.W." The summons to strike makes a reference to the "Wisers far
away," probably those who are more intelligent than we and are
guiding us. The official investigation shows that the Watch Tower
Movement has some influence among the Rhodesian natives.

Watch Tower is a secret society originating in America. It issues political tracts and pamphlets. It has headquarters in Cape
Town and its representatives hold meetings in Rhodesia and
for that matter all over South Africa. The Watch Tower bases its
teaching on the second coming of Christ. Having on previous
occasions foretold the exact date it does not do so any longer, but

it confidently expects Christ and thinks that when he comes the government of the world will be delivered into his hands. This is not very different from the doctrine of the missionaries. But Watch Tower goes on to declare that all the governments which are ruling the world, especially Great Britain and the United States of America, are organizations of Satan, and that all churches, especially the Protestant and Roman Catholic churches, are emissaries of Satan. Religion thus becomes a weapon in the class struggle.

All the Watch Tower books and pamphlets preach a transparent doctrine. The Devil's organization is made up "principally of those that rule and that are called the official part of the nation." Governments are "the Beast," particularly the seventh World Power, which is Great Britain. "The League of Nations is against God and his anointed, but who is primarily responsible for the League of Nations compact"? The Devil is its father, the British Empire its mother. "Catholicism is an abomination in the sight of the Lord, but the Protestants are even more abominable than Catholics." Organized Christianity is full of filthiness, full of "hypocrisy, abomination, fornication and filthiness. Under the present form of government the people suffer much injustice and are greatly oppressed. Their taxes are high, while the products of their labor are low in price. The facts are that a great change from an extremely selfish government to one that is wholly unselfish and righteous is just at hand."

The illustrations preach corresponding sentiments with a greater vigor. One feature for instance displays four people quarreling over a prone body. One is a fat gross European in a dress suit with top hat and hunting crop. The second is a similar figure in a frock coat and with a bag of money. The third is a European apache with a drawn dagger in his hand. The fourth is a fat Bishop with a mitre. Behind is the devil spurring them on. This is supposed to represent Universal War.

It is difficult to say exactly the true influence of the Watch Tower. The writer has been informed by Negro sailors that its influence is widely spread throughout Africa, and that it is the most powerful revolutionary force in Africa today. The gentle Jesus, meek and mild, of the missionaries cannot compete with the Watch Tower God. The Commission which inquired into Rhodesian "disturbances" recognized its importance and devoted many pages to it.

Such are the ideas moving in the minds of these African copper miners. They are absurd only on the surface. They represent political realities and express political aspirations far more closely than program and policies of parties with millions of members, numerous journals and half a century of history behind them. Watch Tower says what the thinking native thinks and what he is prepared to die for.

In his *The Native Problem in Africa,* Dr. Buell makes one very noteworthy observation:

> The extreme credulity with which natives, under the spell of a leader claiming divine or mystical power, will throw away their material interests and recklessly sacrifice their lives is one of the most amazing features of Africa today. The African native is, however, not likely to express this type of fanaticism in a deliberate attack upon European authority. But he has already demonstrated an extraordinary power of passive resistance which will make the problem of control more difficult than if the native population attempted to massacre the Europeans in cold blood.

This apparent fanaticism is the best indication to the true feeling of many millions of Africans. They know what they want, but they do not know what to do. Except in colonies like Sierra Leone and Gambia and to some degree among the Negro intelligentsia of the coastal districts on the West Coast, this passion for liberation must be understood as lying behind every industrial dispute, every political agitation. This is the true Africa. And that is why the whites fear them so much and seek to terrorize them. Dr. Buell wrote over ten years ago. Since then have taken place the Congo revolts already treated which had little or nothing to do with religion. Watch Tower, it should be noted, preaches a fierce resentment against all the imperialist Powers. It does not seek to distinguish between the Fascist and the democratic imperialisms. To the vast body of Africans in Africa such a distinction is meaningless.

The implications of this suppressed but burning resentment reach far. If, for instance, a revolt began in the Congo and spread to South Africa, East Africa, West Africa, the Africans could easily overwhelm the whites if these could no longer receive assistance from abroad. In Nigeria, with a population of twenty millions, there are less than 5,000 white people, and in Lagos, a town of 150,000 people, there are only 1,000 whites. There are many whites in South Africa, which forms a special problem, but the real basis of imperialist control in Africa is the cruisers and airplanes of Europe.

Though often retarded and sometimes diverted, the current of history, observed from an eminence, can be seen to unite strange and diverse tributaries in its own embracing logic. The San Domingo revolutionaries, the black arm in the Civil War, were unconscious but potent levers in two great propulsions forward of modern civilization. Today the Rhodesian copper-miner, living the life of three shillings a week, is but another cog in the wheels of a creaking world economy, as uneconomic in the twentieth century as a naked slave in the cotton-fields of Alabama a hundred years ago. But Negro emancipation has expanded with the centuries; what was local and national in San Domingo and America is today an international urgency, entangling the future of a hundred million Africans with all the hopes and fears of Western Europe. Though dimly, the political consciousness immanent in the historical process emerges in groping and neglected Africa. If Toussaint wrote in the language of '89, the grotesquerie of Watch Tower primitively approximates to the dialectic of Marx and Lenin. This it is which lifts out of bleakness and invests with meaning a record of failure almost unrelieved. The African bruises and breaks himself against his bars in the interest of freedoms wider than his own.

Epilogue

The History of Pan-African Revolt: A Summary, 1939–1969

I have to review the thirty years from 1938 when this book was published to 1969. This involves the social, using the word in the broadest sense, and the political activity, defeats and successes of hundreds of millions of people in Africa; tens of millions in the United States; and a few million in the West Indies who make up in intensity and potentiality for the insignificance of their numbers. Apart from the mere mass of the material, few periods in history exceed, in fact approach, the range of achievement, change, dramatic events and striking personalities of this particular period in history. Under these circumstances it is necessary even, at the cost of a few hundred words, where words are so precious, to make clear what can be done and what cannot be done, in fact to set the tone and the mood in which this review must be approached.

Anatole France (now, alas, low in critical estimation) made many not only witty but wise observations: A famous ruler, after many successes not excluding failures, called together the wise men of his kingdom and told them he wanted them to study and report to him the facts and the understanding of History. The learned old men accepted the responsibility, gathered their assistants and their materials and retired for twenty years. They then returned with twenty volumes in which they had summarized the facts and the significance of History. By this time the monarch was an old man and he complained: "How do you expect me at my age to cope with all that, to read far less to study twenty large volumes? Go away, summarize the twenty volumes so that I will be able to read them." The historians went away and after twenty years one very old man with a long beard returned with a single volume. "Sire," he said, "my fellow scholars are all dead. I have summarized it all and here it is in one volume." The monarch lay on what he knew to be his death bed, and he bitterly complained. "You mean to say that I will never know the facts and the significance of History? How can I read even that large single volume which you bring to me?" The old historian put the book aside and told him: "Sire, I can summarize the history of man for you so that you can understand it before you die: They were born, they suffered, they died."

I wish my readers to understand the history of Pan-African Revolt during the last thirty years. They fought, they suffered—they are still fighting. Once we understand that, we can tackle our problems with the necessary mental equilibrium.

First Africa: I shall take only two of the nearly fifty African States, which have won their independence or increased their powers. The first is what we know today as Ghana, the second is Kenya. It helps that I have known personally the national leaders of both countries.

I. Africa

Gold Coast to Ghana

There lived in Accra a sub-chief called Nii Kwabena Bonne III. He was also a businessman. He made a short campaign through the country enlisting the support of the Chiefs. He then, on January 11, 1948, called a boycott on the purchase of European imported goods. The boycott was as complete as such an undertaking could be. It became general in the Colony and Ashanti and lasted until the February 24.

During the boycott events of immense symbolical significance took place. Native administrations, up to this point, like the Chiefs, tools of the Government, now used their legal position to impose fines upon those who did not cooperate in the boycott of European goods. Groups of young men went around the towns maintaining the boycott by force when necessary.

It was only on February 11 that the Government intervened. There was a series of meetings between the Chamber of Commerce and Nii Bonne III, with the Colonial Secretary in the Chair. It was agreed that prices should be lowered for a trial period of three months. Nii Bonne III then called off the boycott.

Meanwhile, the Ex-Servicemen's Union planned to present a petition to the Governor setting forth their grievances on Monday, the February 24, 1948, but they postponed it until Saturday the 28th. On that day the Ex-Servicemen's Union began their march. In the course of it they changed the prescribed route and announced their determination to march on Christiansborg Castle, the residence of the Governor. They found a squad of police in their way and in the course of the dispute which followed, the Superintendent of Police, a white man, fired at the ringleaders, killed two of them and wounded four or five. The news spread into the industrial district of Accra where the people for the first time in a month were buying European goods. They were already dissatisfied because they believed that the goods were not being sold to them at the prices stated in the published agreement, which had preceded the calling off of the boycott. The news of the shooting precipitated an outburst of rage. The

people attacked the European shops and looted them. The police were unable to restore order for two days, Saturday the 28th
and Sunday the 29th. There was destruction of property by fire
and in the two days fifteen persons were killed and 115 injured
in Accra alone: There were other disturbances in various parts
of the Colony. The most important were at Koforidua where the
outbreak began after the arrival of a lorry with men from Accra.
They broke out in Kumasi and district on Monday, March 1st, an
hour after the arrival of the train from Accra.

Nkrumah says that he and his organization, the United Gold
Coast Convention, had nothing whatever to do with the disturbances, and, as we shall see, there is every reason to believe him.

These are the bare facts of the case. When, however, we look
a little more closely in the light of after-events, an often analyzed
logical movement discloses itself. These were no ordinary riots
of a hungry populace over high prices. The first stage of every
revolution is marked by a great mass movement of the populace, usually led by representatives of the old order. M. Georges
Lefebvre of that great school of historians, the French historians of the French Revolution, has established that the bourgeois
revolution in France in 1789 was preceded by mass rioting during what he calls the "crisis of the monarchy" which took place in
1788, one year before the popular eruption which captured the
Bastille on July 14, 1789.[52] In this case we are in the middle of the
twentieth century.

The first outburst takes the form of an economic boycott
that lasted a month, but it is led by a Chief and supported by
the Chiefs. The people of Accra follow exactly the course that
the masses of the people have followed in every great revolution. The only organization at hand was the organization of
ex-servicemen, and when they began their march they were at
once reinforced by large numbers of spectators and sympathizers. Whatever had been the original intention of the ex-servicemen, these sympathizers encouraged them to take the road to
the Governor's Castle. Anti-racial cries were frequently uttered.

---

52. A few words here were omitted from earlier editions. See Publisher's
Foreword.

Among the remarks were such as "This is the last European Governor who will occupy the Castle." (They were not far wrong; he was the last but one.) The crowd directed a heavy fusillade of stones against the police. When the police tried to stop them, they shouted insults at the European officers and invited the Africans in the ranks to abandon their duty. It seems that they were successful. For when the Superintendent finally gave the order to fire, the Africans did not shoot and he himself had to seize a rifle from the nearest man to fire the shots which caused the casualties. Superintendent Imray had with him at the time only ten men. The idea that a crowd of 2,000, many of them men who had seen battle, was cowed by the shooting is ridiculous. They could have swept the ten men away in ten seconds, and as there was only two officers and twenty men at Christiansborg, the Castle could easily have become another Bastille. In these situations you have to work by inferences, similar conjunctures in previous historical situations and an absence of prejudice against crowds and against Africans. The crowd retreated because it realized that to sweep away the petty resistance which faced it would be to initiate a battle for which it knew it was not prepared. Therefore, as crowds will do under such circumstances, it preferred to retreat.

I am here using the report of the investigations made later by a Colonial Office Commission, and it must be remembered first that at moments like these what the crowd is really thinking and the motives of its actions are profoundly difficult to recapture after the actions have taken place; and in any case a Government Commission is not exactly the body which would know whom to question, how to elicit the answers that matter, and even to understand what evidence it does manage to collect. The Commission calls the crowd a "lawless mob." That was precisely what it was not. It was acting instinctively according to certain fundamental laws of revolution and we shall see that it obeys these laws to the very end.

We should note these incipient actions carefully because, unless there is a great unsettlement of the settled policy of His Majesty's Government and the other European powers, that is precisely what is going to take place over vast areas of colonial Africa. What has really taken place can be summed up as follows:

1. The people on a national scale have mobilized and organized themselves during the boycott and felt their power, and they have been able to do so rapidly because this first step is taken under their traditional leaders, their Chiefs.

2. The call to the African police not to obey their European officers and not to shoot was not an accident. It takes place at the beginning of all revolutions. Neither was it spontaneous. Already, during the boycott, at the trial of a local chief on a charge arising out of the enforcement of the boycott, posters had appeared in Accra calling upon the police to strike and to refuse to obey the orders of the European officers.

3. The march on Christiansborg Castle and the shouts that the Governor would be the last European governor show that out of the confidence built up in the month-long boycott, the people had proclaimed the ultimate slogan of the revolution, the end of imperial rule.

They knew what they wanted. If they turned aside from the direct march to the Castle and hesitated before sweeping aside the police, it was because they understood the consequences of such actions. They had been waiting for somebody to lead them and they welcomed Nkrumah as a person to do so. Lawless mob indeed. Within eighteen months Nkrumah was going to call a Ghana Constituent Assembly in Accra, which would be attended by 90,000 people. Within two years these people would carry out a policy of Positive Action in which the life of the whole country would be brought to a standstill with the utmost discipline and order. Within three years they would give Nkrumah a vote of 22,780 out of a possible 23,122.

Nkrumah was taken out of jail to be made Leader of Government Business. Then after years of in-fighting he finally achieved the independence of the Gold Coast in 1957.

The Myth of Mau Mau

Not African beliefs and tribal practices but land and white settlers on the land were to be decisive in shaping the character of the black revolt in Kenya. The railway made possible the export of cash crops by Europeans settled on the fertile temperate land of the Kenya Highlands. A policy of encouraging white settlement, a new policy in Africa, soon received the official blessing of the Foreign Office. Subsequently, under Colonial Office supervision, European settlement rapidly became the most powerful influence in the social, economic, and political development of the new country.

It was in the first decade of the twentieth century that this new Kenya took shape. One of the largest early applications for land (500 square miles) was made in April 1902 by the East Africa Syndicate, a company with a strong South African interest. With only a dozen settlers established at the beginning of 1903, in August the Commissioner, Sir Charles Eliot, sent his Collector of Customs, A. Marsden, to South Africa to encourage settlers to migrate to the country. By the end of 1905 over a million acres of land had been leased or sold by the Protectorate authorities. In 1906 a large party of Boer "Irreconcilables" trekked overland from the Transvaal to the Kenya highlands; others poured in by boat from Britain and South Africa.

Thus began something new in an African colony: the struggle to make it a "white man's country."

Nowhere in Africa was there such a struggle as began before 1914 and lasted decade after decade until it culminated in the independence of Kenya nearly fifty years later. Between 1903 and 1906 important areas of Kikuyu land were alienated. Some 8,000 shillings was paid in compensation to 8,000 Kikuyu, but more than 3,000 received nothing at all. Commissioner Eliot was to write that "no one can doubt that the rich and exceptionally fertile district of Kikuyu is destined to be one of the chief centers of European cultivation, and the process of settlement is facilitated by the fact that there are gaps where there is no native population."

By 1914, the exclusive "White Highlands" was already a reality, and the Europeans were demanding the conventional right of British colonists to elect their own representatives to the Protectorate's Legislative Council.

The struggle was continuous. Ultimately (by the early 1950s) the Africans, mainly but not entirely Kikuyu, took to arms, and from encampments and hiding places in the forests raided settled establishments and slew white farmers and those Africans who supported the British regime. Dedan Kimathi and Waruhiu Itote ("General China") were generally acknowledged as the senior leaders of the nationalist armies. Food, funds, arms, medical supplies could be secured only by immense risks and labors. In some parts the Home Guard was strong, in others weak. In some areas the chief was sympathetic, in others he was a dedicated "loyalist." There were some wonderful leaders whose names ought to be recorded—Kimathi himself, Stanley Mathenge, China, and Tanganyika in Nyeri, Matenjagwo, Kago, and Mbaria Kaniu in Fort Hall, and Kimbo, the cattle-raider, operating between Nanyuki and Maivasha. The difficult terrain prevented easy lateral communication within the forest itself, and the campaign soon developed into a series of local battles of attrition, ridge by ridge.

Though defeated in the Reserves, and with some surrendering to the British Security Forces, nonetheless many men and women in the forest continued their resistance. Their aim, apart from surviving and carrying on the struggle for land and freedom, was to attract international attention to their cause. No outside help was forthcoming, and the Emergency did not give rise to a major political investigating commission from Britain.

From 1953 to 1955, Kimathi sought to provide an overall perspective of the resistance in the forest. At one point, while in the forest, Kimathi was reported to have said: "I do not lead rebels but I lead Africans who want their self-government and land. My people want to live in a better world than they met with when they were born. I lead them because God never created a true and real brotherhood between white and black so that we may be regarded as people and as human beings who can do each and every thing."

Yet the plain fact is that the nationalist army in the forests was defeated by the huge forces sent by the British Government to maintain the colonial regime. Some 50,000 Kikuyu and other revolutionaries were detained in special camps to undergo special training to cure them of the mental disease which the British authorities discovered as the cause of their refusal to submit. Jomo Kenyatta was given a long prison sentence and, having served it, was confined far away from the center of Kenya politics.

Despite this reconstitution of physical and military authority the British found that they could no longer govern the people of Kenya. Constitutional manipulation and constitutional maneuver were worked out, agreed upon by the British Parliament and its experts, only to meet rejection and failure. In the end Kenya had to be granted political independence. The stories spread about "Mau Mau" have been exposed for the anti-African myths that they are. There is nothing inherently African about "Mau Mau." Their social organization and corresponding beliefs being broken up and persecuted by the British, what was (by the British) labeled as Mau Mau was an *ad hoc* body of beliefs, oaths, disciplines newly created for the specific purpose of gathering and strengthening the struggle against British imperialism, its military, political and economic domination and, in particular, the Christianity it sought to inject and impose.

Independence and After

In the Gold Coast and in Kenya we have the two extremes of the African struggles for independence. Nothing in modern history was more starting than the rapidity with which other African states achieved political independence. In Algeria the French imperialists had an experience similar to the Kenya experience. The French military had established what they considered military power over the necessarily not-well-organized Algerian nationalist forces. They believed that they had established control over the political resistance. They engineered General de Gaulle into power in France in order finally to teach Algerians that they were French. But the General understood a revolutionary upheaval better than they did. He realized that whatever the strength of guns and of prisons, the colonial mentality of accepting domination was broken and could never be restored. To the fury of the French imperialists and army he worked out an independence agreement with the Algerian nationalists, saving what he could for French finance and capital. Such was the disappointment and anger of the French generals in particular that they tried to assassinate him. So blatant was their attempt that some of them had to be tried and even jailed. Such was the naked proof of the rapacity of that small section of the population of an advanced civilization, which profited by imperialism. Similarly, thousands of Frenchmen who had lived well by exploiting the Algerian people left Algeria and returned to France.

The murder of Lumumba and the tireless efforts of the late Tshombe dramatized the attempt by Belgian imperialism to maintain its exploitation of the vast mineral wealth of the Congo, while giving some token recognition to the irresistible movement for national independence.

The dozen years that have unfolded since the winning of independence by the Gold Coast in 1957 are some of the most far-ranging and politically intense that history has known. African state after African state has gained political independence with a tumultuous rush that was not envisaged even by the most sanguine of the early advocates of independence. The names of leaders obscure the political reality. What is to be noted is that Kenyatta, Nkrumah, Banda, to take the best-known names, were all imprisoned by the British Government and *had to be released to head the independent states.* The British Government, as did the French and Belgian, found that despite their soldiers, their guns and planes, they could not rule. The colonial mentality having been broken, the only way to restore some sort of order or, to reject a word now corrupted and offensive, the only way to have a viable society was to transfer the man in jail to be the head of state. In no other way could the African people once more accommodate themselves to any social structure.

They accepted the African leader and his African colleagues. But that is precisely why in African state after African state, with almost the rapidity with which independence was gained, military dictatorship after military dictatorship has succeeded to power, the most depressing of all being the overthrow of what had appeared to be the most progressive and successful of the new African governments—the government of Mali. What are the reasons for this rapid decay and decline of African nationalism? The best known and the reason most often advanced by Africans and advocates of African independence is the continued exploitation by the industrial and finance-capital of Europe and the United States. Even people no more than casually informed are aware of the continual lowering of the prices of the commodities, most often single-crop or unit-minerals, produced by the African countries, and the raising of the prices of the manufactured goods needed by the newly independent African countries in their necessarily frantic efforts to modernize themselves. Banks, and old industries with new African names working through local agents (such as the East Indian community in Kenya), continue to control the life of the newly independent African communities. "Aid," so small in quantity and so large in publicity, would gladly be dispensed with, if economic independence were automatically to result from political independence.

However, without minimizing the continuing economic subordination of the newly independent African states, there are objective reasons for the apparent decline, in fact abrupt disintegration and resort to crude military dictatorship in African state after African state.

The states which the African nationalist leaders inherited were not in any sense African. With the disintegration of the political power of the imperialist states in Africa, and the rise of militancy of the African masses, a certain political pattern took shape. Nationalist political leaders built a following, they or their opponents gained support among the African civil servants who had administered the imperialist state, and the newly independent African state was little more than the old imperialist state only now administered and controlled by black nationalists. That these men, western-educated and western-oriented, had or would have little that was nationalist or African to contribute to the establishment of a truly new and truly African order was seen most clearly by the late Frantz Fanon, and he established his still constantly increasing reputation by his untrammeled advocacy of revolt against these black nationalist regimes. Uncompromising revolt he saw as the only means of ridding Africa of the economic and psychological domination by Western civilization which, independence or no independence, seemed certain to keep Africa and Africans hewers of wood and drawers of water to Western civilization. Sekou Toure of Guinea seemed to be the only African leader who aimed at building a society which would use European techniques to strengthen and develop the African heritage. But not only was Guinea a very small and very underdeveloped state, but the Moscow assistants whom he hoped would help him, plotted to overthrow his regime and Guinea did not make the progress which would set an example for Africa. That example, however, was to come from Tanzania, under the leadership of Dr. Nyerere. The impact that the policies of Tanzania has made upon Africa and can in time make upon the rest of the world, underdeveloped or advanced, has already established the African state of Tanzania as one of the foremost political phenomena of the twentieth century. Tanzania is the highest peak reached so far by revolting blacks and it is imperative to make clear, not least of all to blacks everywhere, the new stage of political thought which has been reached. But first to establish some idea of what is happening in other areas of Negro political reality and response since 1938.

II. South Africa

Since the end of World War II nowhere has any regime in the world (or for that matter any modern historical regime) made it more clear what is its primary and permanent concern. This preoccupation is the repression and containment of the increasing revolutionary rejection of its exploitation and oppression by the millions of blacks on whose backs it lives and thrives. Such is the record which the South African regime of whites daily registers in contemporary history aided by the benevolent neutrality of Europe and America, and the border states that it seeks to build and strengthen against political destruction by a self-conscious independent African continent.

All that will be attempted here is to give what is usually neglected, the pressure—the objective social pressure—which the South African blacks, the most highly developed in Africa, exercise on the very vitals of the South African regime.

A Prime Minister of South Africa, Mr. B.J. Vorster, made it absolutely clear that the regime had no intention of giving political rights to urban Africans. Speaking in Parliament on April 24, 1968, he said:

> They remain there because they cannot provide employment for themselves. But the fact that you employ those people, does not place you under any obligation to grant them political rights in your parliament. Surely the fact that you work for a man does not give you the right to run his affairs? . . . It is true that there are blacks working for us. They will continue to work for us for generations, in spite of the ideal we have to separate them completely. . . .
>
> The fact of the matter is this; we need them, because they work for us, but, after all, we pay them for their work. . . . But the fact that they work for us can never entitle them to claim political rights. Not now, nor in the future . . . under no circumstances can we grant them those political rights in our own territory, neither now nor never.

That indicates the fear that white South Africa has of the blacks.

Any examination of South Africa's labor laws and policies will show the pretense and the reality of the status of Africans in the urban areas. More than 4,000,000 Africans live in the urban areas. In spite of desperate measures to limit the flow of Africans into the towns, the urban African population doubled between 1945 and 1960, when 3,471,233 were counted in the census. For twelve of those remarkable fifteen years, the Nationalist government was busily engaged in applying its policy of keeping the races apart.

For better appreciation of the situation, one should study the racial composition of the thirteen principal urban areas, listed in the accompanying table. These centers of industrial and commercial activity have been designated "white" areas although their white population is far less than their non-white.

The greatest concentration of industry is on the Witwatersrand, where there are twice as many non-whites as whites and Africans alone outnumber whites by over half-a-million.

Population of Principal Urban Areas 1960 (Approximate)

	Africans	Whites	Coloreds	Asians
Johannesburg	650,912	413,153	59,467	28,993
Cape Town	75,200	305,155	417,881	8,975
Durban	221,535	196,398	27,082	236,477

The purpose of the Urban Areas Act is to control the influx of Africans into the urban areas; to set apart areas for their accommodation; to direct their labor; and to impose strict regulations for their control and movement. In short, it aims at providing whites with black labor without allowing blacks to acquire residential, social and other rights in the areas where they are employed. Try as they will, the South African whites cannot isolate or circumscribe the black population. The simple truth is that without the participation of the black population the South African economy would fall apart.

Here are some figures, published by the Anti-Apartheid Movement in February 1969.

Population (mid-1967)

	Numbers	Percentage
Africans	12 ¾ million	68
Whites	3 ½ million	19
Coloreds	1 ¾ million	10
Indians	½ million	3

88 percent of Coloured people live in the Cape.

83 percent of the Indian people in the Natal. They are debarred from living on the Orange Free State.

Distribution of population by race in each of the four largest cities (percent)

	Whites	Africans	Coloreds	Indians
Johannesburg	36	56	5	3
Cape Town	38	9	52	1
Durban	29	32	4	35
Pretoria	49	47	2	2

There have been created three so-called African states, Transkei, Ciskei and Tswanaland, labeled Bantustans so as to create some sense of race and nation separate from white South Africa. That cannot alter nor mitigate the remorseless pressures of the blacks of South Africa against the whites. The imprisonings, the tortures and the shootings now have been met by guerrilla warfare substantially authenticated. One thing is certain. The existing regime in South Africa can continue to exist only by the increasing persecution and brutal repression of the existing blacks. History in general, and the particulars of this history, indicate a violent end to this regime sooner or later, and sooner rather than later.

III. The United States

1952 was the first year in seventy-one years that there were no lynchings. But that does not mean that the bodies of black men who had offended whites were no longer found floating in shallow waters, or that at times black men disappeared, their relations and friends uncertain whether they had gone North or had been liquidated by white racists. The National Association for the Advancement of Colored People, a predominantly middle-class organization, chiefly of blacks but including sympathetic whites, concentrated on the abolition of legal discrimination against Negroes and earned notable successes. Legal struggles and mass action reacted on each other. The famous bus boycott in Montgomery, Alabama, began on December 5, 1955, and this action, of a range and solidity unprecedented, unloosed a flood which became a torrent. On June 5, 1956, a Federal court ruled that racial segregation on Montgomery city buses violated the Constitution. Later that year, the Supreme Court upheld a lower court decision which banned segregation on Montgomery buses. Federal injunctions prohibiting this segregation were served on city, state and bus company officials on December 20. At mass meetings, Montgomery blacks called off the year-long bus boycott, and buses were integrated on December 21.

Congress passed the Civil Rights Act of 1957, the first federal civil rights legislation since 1875. That very year. President Eisenhower, with obvious reluctance to take such a step, ordered federal troops to Little Rock, Arkansas, to prevent interference with school integration at Central High School. That was on September 24. These episodes might have seemed to be merely unusual types of struggles which in the past had been halfheartedly projected or even attempted. Rapidly they showed themselves to be precipitants of the greatest social crisis the United States had known since the Civil War.

It was black students who initiated this struggle. On February 1, 1960 four students from a North Carolina college started a sit-in movement at Greensboro, North Carolina, in a five and dime store. By February 10 the movement had spread to fifteen Southern cities in five states. In March, one thousand Alabama State students marched on the State Capitol and held a protest meeting. In April the Student Nonviolent Coordinating Committee was organized on the Shaw University campus. In May, President Eisenhower signed the Civil Rights Act of 1960, but that was insignificant in comparison with the tremendous movement that now began among blacks: the masses of the population in city after city; the groups of "Freedom Riders"—black young men and women who faced the bombs, bullets, whips and prisons of the South, official and unofficial; the black students on the campuses; black youths in the schools. Let it not be forgotten that both the New Left and the revolutionary defiance of campus authority by white students began to take shape as a direct result of the black students turning from protests by asking for reforms to protests by revolutionary action.

It would be a mistake here to attempt to give details about either events or personalities. Even to name some is to omit and thereby discriminate against others. It may be said, however, that names such as LeRoi Jones, Stokely Carmichael, Eldridge Cleaver, Rap Brown, Malcolm X, Martin Luther King, the Black Panthers, are household names not only among young people in the United States but among white populations all over the world. Summer after summer has seen tremendous struggles by the black masses, led by unknown, obscure, local leaders. Perhaps the most significant was that which followed the assassination of Dr. Martin Luther King, the world-famous black leader. The American government placed a cordon of troops around the White House and government buildings and areas in Washington. They then abandoned the city, the capital of the United States, to the embittered and insurgent blacks, who constitute a majority of the Washington population. The question to be asked: what else could the government have done?

One can only record the question most often and most seriously asked: can any government mobilize the white population, or a great majority of it, in defense of white racism against militant blacks? The only legitimate answer lies in the continuing militancy or retreat of the black population. This population is at least 30 million in number, strategically situated in the heart of many of the most important cities in the United States. If the black population continues to resist racism, the militants and youth actively and the middle classes sympathetic or neutral, then the physical defeat of the black struggle against racism will involve the destruction of the United States as it has held together since 1776.

IV. The Caribbean

The Caribbean is a small area where British and French have ruled for centuries and where at the present one or two British territories have been granted what is known as independence. There are a few points that are to be made about these extraordinarily significant but on the world scale minute territories.

First of all, it is only recently that a British scholar, Sir Richard Pares, in a work called *Merchants and Planters*, has made it clear that as far back as the middle of the eighteenth century the slaves actually ran the plantations—those plantations that were the source of so much wealth, which contributed so substantially to the advancement of the advanced countries. *Merchants and Planters* is a study of the Caribbean and was published for the Economic History Society at the Cambridge University Press. Pares notes that:

> in all the inventories which are to be found among the West Indian archives it is very usual for the mill, the cauldron, the still and the buildings to count for more than one-sixth of the total capital; in most plantations one-tenth would be nearer the mark. By far the greatest capital items were the value of the slaves and the acreage planted in canes by their previous labor.

So that the greatest capital value (about 1760) of the sugar plantations, was the labor of the slaves and the acres they had planted. All sorts of economists do all sorts of studies about the West Indies but they don't know that the real value of those precious economic units was the slaves and the land they had developed by their labors. This escapes nearly all, except this English scholar.

Pares goes on to say: "Yet, when we look closely, we find that the industrial capital required was much larger than a sixth of the total value. With the mill, the boiling house and the still went an army of specialists—almost all of them slaves, but none the less specialists for that."

There was an army of slaves, but they were specialists. This tremendous economy that made so much wealth, particularly for British society—it was the slaves who ran those plantations. Pares drives home the point: "They were not only numerous but, because of their skill, they had a high value. If we add their cost to that of the instruments and machinery which they used, we find that the industrial capital of the plantations without which it could not be a plantation at all, was probably not much less than half its total capital."

Pares obviously feels it imperative to reiterate what he no doubt has failed to find in previous studies. "But when we examine specifications of the Negroes, we find so many boilers, masons, carters, boatswains of the mill, etc., that we cannot feel much confidence in our categories, especially when we find individuals described as 'excellent boiler and field Negro'"

So that about 1766 Negroes ran the plantations. A man is described as an excellent boiler and field Negro, but this prevents us from putting such persons on either side of the line. He not only worked in the fields but also did the necessary technical work. Further complication arises from the fact that specialist jobs were awarded to the sickly and the ruptured. The sickly or the ruptured were given the technical jobs to do—we have to look afresh at the rapid spread of technical skill.

That gives an entirely different picture of the kind of civilization that was in existence in the West Indies well before the French Revolution of 1789. In the United States in general skilled labor was the preserve of whites. There were no white laborers in the Caribbean. There is other evidence elsewhere and it seems legitimate to say that the slaves ran the society. If they had been removed the society would have collapsed. That in fact is perfectly clear in certain writings about Trinidad and Tobago.

This is the process whereby the inhabitants of these Caribbean islands have made an astonishing mastery of the techniques of Western civilization. Race prejudice, however, continues to be subtly, and not so subtly, a dominant feature of the social structure of the islands. What has happened is that the population, without any native background (the Amerindians were all wiped out), have been compelled to master the languages and the techniques of Western civilization which they have done with astonishing skill. The struggle for African and black independence is studded with distinguished individuals of Caribbean origin: Rene Maran, winner of the Prix Goncourt in 1921 for his exposure in his novel *Batouala* of French degradation of the African peoples in Africa, where be worked as a civil servant; Marcus Garvey, George Padmore, Frantz Fanon, Aime Cesaire, Stokely Carmichael . . . But this mastery of certain aspects of Western civilization has been able to exercise itself fully only in Western Europe and the United States for the imperialists continue, as they have done from the beginning, to dominate the economic and finances of the territories. The only difference today is that black men administer the imperialist interests. The situation is highly explosive. Whereas the economy continues to be a coloni- alist economy of the seventeenth century, completely dominated by foreign powers, the population is a modern population, a population of the twentieth century, learned in the languages and techniques of Western civilization and highly developed because of the smallness of the islands and the close relations between what is technically known as urban and rural. A federation was attempted in the British islands, the British being anxious to rid themselves of the responsibility of these islands, the Caribbean being now an American sea. But the federation fell apart. The reason is very simple: A federation meant that the economic line of direction should no longer be from each island to London, pre- viously the financial and economic capital of each territory. The new lines of direction should have been from island to island. But this involved the break-up of the old colonial system. The West Indian politicians preferred the break-up of the federation.

What is the situation in the islands, what is inherent there and what may break out at any minute, is proved by the revolt that has in 1969 broken out in the island of Curafao, dominated by Dutch oil interests.

The revolt was a revolt of workers and unemployed youth and they burned down business houses of a value variously estimated between 15 and 40 millions (Dutch money). On the surface the revolt was a spontaneous process against Westcar, a sub-contrac- tor of Shell Oil, who lowered salaries and laid off workers. But the ensuing strike spread to Shell, representing more than 90 percent of the national income. The workers marched on Parliament and when the marchers clashed with a column of armed police the eruption broke out.

Meanwhile, 300 political prisoners are in the penitentiary. According to local law, they can be kept there if need be for two years while their cases are being investigated.

Nominally "peace" would have been achieved by the arrival of 600 Dutch marines, but not in 1969. An uneasy peace was really secured by the resignation of the Democratic Government which had been in power for fourteen years. Facing a Revolution, it has agreed to hold elections. It is freely stated by leaders of the Working

Class Front that if the Democratic Government is re-elected, the events of May will be repeated with even greater devastation.

Herbert Specer, President of the Federation of Petroleum Workers, states what is the obvious truth: "In the last analysis the significance of the May revolt is that people want change, and if they don't get it anything could happen." Small as they are, their historical origin and development have been such that these Caribbean islands can make highly significant contributions to the economics and politics of a world in torment. That is exactly what Castro's Cuba has done.

V. "Always Out of Africa"

For many hundreds of years, in fact almost (though not quite) from the beginning of the contact between Western civilization and Africa, it has been the almost universal practice to treat African achievement, discoveries and creations as if Western civilization was the norm and the African people spent their years in imitating, trying to reach or, worse still, if necessary going through the primitive early stages of the Western world. We therefore will, before we place it historically, state as straightforwardly as possible the historical achievements that are taking place today in an African state.

First the Tanzanian Government has nationalized the chief centers of economic life in the territory. That though important and necessary is not sufficient to create a new society. Less and less is nationalization becoming a landmark of a new society—today right-wing military dictators (Peru) and the Catholic hierarchy (with the blessing of the Pope) are ready to nationalize and even confiscate. The Government of Tanzania has gone further. In the Arusha Declaration of 29 January 1967 it aims at treating a new type of government official:

PART FIVE: THE ARUSHA RESOLUTION

Therefore, the National Executive Committee, meeting in the Community center at Arusha from 26.1.67 to 29.1.67, resolves:

A. *The Leadership*

Every TANU and Government leader must be either a Peasant or a Worker, and should in no way
be associated with the practices of Capitalism or
Feudalism.

No TANU or Government leader should hold shares
in any company.

No TANU or Government leader should hold
Directorship in any privately-owned enterprises.

No TANU or Government leader should receive two
or more salaries.

No TANU or Government leader should own houses
which he rents to others.

For the purposes of this Resolution the term
"leader" should comprise the following: Members
of the TANU National Executive Committee;
Ministers, Members of Parliament, Senior Officials
of organizations affiliated to TANU, Senior Officials
of Para-Statal organizations, all those appointed or
elected under any clause of the TANU Constitution,
Councilors, and Civil Servants in high and middle
cadres. (In this context "leader" means a man, or a
man and his wife; a woman, or a woman and her
husband).

Such a resolution would probably exclude 90 percent of
those who govern and administer in other parts of the world,
developed or underdeveloped. The Government aims at creat-
ing a new type of society, based not on Western theories but on
the concrete circumstances of African life and its historic past.

Perhaps the most revolutionary change of all, it will reconstruct the very system of education in order to fit the children
and the youth, in particular the youth in secondary education,
for the new society which the Government of Tanzania seeks
to build. The simplicity with which Dr. Nyerere states what his
government proposes to do disguises the fact that not in Plato

or Aristotle, Rousseau or Karl Marx will you find such radical, such revolutionary departures from the established educational order.

Alongside this change in the approach to the curriculum there must be a parallel and integrated change in the way our schools are run, so as to make them and their inhabitants a real part of our society and our economy. Schools must, in fact, become communities—and communities which practice the precept of self-reliance. The teachers, workers, and pupils together must be the members of a social unit in the same way as parents, relatives, and children are the family social unit. There must be the same kind of relationship between pupils and teachers within the school community as there is between children and parents in the village. And the former community must realize, just as the latter do, that their life and well-being depend upon the production of wealth— by farming or other activities.

This means that all schools, but especially secondary schools and other forms of higher education, must contribute to their own upkeep; they must be economic communities as well as social and educational communities. Each school should have, as an integral part of it, a farm or workshop which provides the food eaten by the community, and makes some contribution to the total national income.

This is not a suggestion that a school farm or workshop should be attached to every school for training purposes. It is a suggestion that every school should also be a farm; that the school community should consist of people who are both teachers and farmers, and pupils and farmers. Obviously, if there is a school farm, the pupils working on it should be learning the techniques and tasks of farming. But the farm would be an integral part of the school and the welfare of the pupils would depend on its output, just as the welfare of a farmer depends on the output of his land. Thus, when this scheme is in operation, the revenue side of school accounts would not just read as

at present: "Grant from Government . . . ; Grant from
voluntary agency or other charity . . ." They would
read: "Income from sale of cotton (or whatever other
cash crop was appropriate for the area) . . . ; Value of
the food grown and consumed . . . ; Value of labor
done by pupils on new building, repairs, equipment,
etc. . . . ; Government subvention . . . ; Grant from . . ."

Perhaps nothing shows more clearly the radical, the revolutionary, the complete break with Western habits and Western
thought than the new attitude to the Tanzanian farmer. Some
of them have followed the advice given to the African farmer
officially and unofficially by Westerners: wishing him and his
country well, they have encouraged him to individual effort, essentially capitalistic. Following this advice farmers in certain districts of Tanzania (mainly the slopes of the Kavirondo Mountain)
have followed this Western type of agriculture with success. Note
now the economic, in fact the political attitude of the Tanzanian
Government to this type of farmer. Reviewing Tanzania "After
the Arusha Declaration" Dr. Nyerere outlines the cooperative socialist community Tanzania aims at. He continues:

> This is the objective. It is stated clearly, and at greater
> length, in the policy paper. We must understand it so
> that we know what we are working towards. But it is
> not something we shall achieve overnight. We have a
> long way to go.
>
> For what has been happening over recent years is
> quite different. We have not been enlarging and mod-
> ernizing our traditional family unit as much as aban-
> doning it in favor of small-scale capitalist farming.
> Many of our most dynamic and energetic farmers, es-
> pecially those with the most initiative and willingness
> to learn new techniques, have been branching out on
> their own as individuals. They have not been enlarg-
> ing their farms by joining with others in a spirit of
> equality, but by employing labor. So we are getting the
> beginnings of the development of an agricultural la-
> boring class on the one hand, and a wealthier employ-
> ing class on the other. Fortunately, this development

has not gone very far; we can arrest the trend without difficulty. But we must not make this change by persecuting the progressive farmers; after all, we have been encouraging them in the direction they have been going! Instead we must seek their cooperation, and integrate them into the new socialist agriculture by showing them that their best interests will be served by this development. For energy and initiative such as these farmers have displayed will be very important to our progress. We need these people.

This is something new in the history of political thought. The cooperative villages aimed at are called Ujamaa and Dr. Nyerere has called the whole new attempt to create a new society Socialism. In our view he is entitled to do so, and a proper respect for what the Tanzanian Government is doing demands that it be related to traditional and contemporary concepts of socialism.

First of all, no one today believes that what exists in Russia and Eastern Europe is, in any sense of the word, socialist; that is to say, a society having achieved and aiming at even more comprehensive stages of liberty, equality and fraternity, social relations higher than those achieved by the most advanced parliamentary democracy. That is socialism, or it is worse even than capitalist decay being then a deliberate and conscious fraud. Worse still, most unfortunately, certain of the new African states, anxious to rid themselves of the capitalist stigma, have invented a new category labeled African socialism. Worthy of repetition is the exposition of this African socialism by one newly independent state.

Adaptability

15. African Socialism must be flexible because the problems it will confront and the incomes and desires of the people will change over time, often quickly and substantially. A rigid, doctrinaire system will have little chance for survival. The system must:

(i) make progress towards ultimate objectives; and

(ii) solve more immediate problems with efficiency.

16. No matter how pressing immediate problems may
be, progress toward ultimate objectives will be the
major consideration. In particular, political equality,
social justice and human dignity will not be sacrificed
to achieve more material ends more quickly. Nor will
these objectives be comprised today in the faint hope
that by so doing they can be reinstated more fully in
some unknown and far distant future.

Whenever was there a state, beginning with the state of Adam
and Eve, that did not, could not, proclaim that it had in mind
ultimate objectives while paying attention to immediate needs?
That is not socialism. It is nonsense. It is not African. It is bureaucratic balderdash, to which we are now well accustomed in
advanced as well as in underdeveloped fakers—a bold attempt by
newcomers to dress the old reality in new clothes.

Far more important than this fakery is the recognition by
President Kaunda of Zambia that the attempt merely to ape
European ways, which has brought such wide fields of disaster to
Africa, must not only be rejected but that there are new African
paths to be explored. In his significantly named "Humanism in
Zambia" President Kaunda says:

> This is a key point, for if the distribution of wealth is not
> done properly, it might lead to the creation of classes in
> society and the much-valued humanist approach that
> is traditional and inherent in our African society would
> have suffered a final blow. If this happened the world
> as a whole, and African in particular, would be all the
> poorer for it. For you would then have the "haves" and
> the "have-nots." Politically you would be creating room
> for opposing parties based on "the oppressed" and
> "the oppressor" concept which again would not be in
> keeping with the society described above; a society in
> which the Chief as an elected or appointed leader of the
> people held national property like land in trust for the
> people, and he was fully aware that he was responsible
> to them. He knew, too, that his continuing to be their
> head depended on his people's will.

President Kaunda wants to show how important it is for Africans to break cleanly with the ideas of European well-wishers, that African progress depends on educating first a small number of Africans and then an increasing number who will gradually (without undue haste) educate more and more African natives to capitalist energies and the moderate mastery of parliamentary democracy. His rejection of this concept is total.

> Now we must ask again what effects will persistently increasing levels of specialization have on our much valued traditional society in our country. This field of specialization drives people to resort to new groups in society. In other words, people with common interests group together, partly because of the community of their interests and partly as the means of promoting and protecting the welfare of their group. For example, a carpenter will find his own interests are not the same as those of the commercial farmer. The teacher finds that his interests differ from those of the mine worker. And so the whole list of different interests can be outlined. This point is, all this gives birth to a new disintegrative tendency. This, as can be seen, cuts right across the traditional society which has been described above as a mutual aid society which was an accepting and inclusive community.

Despite the low-level of economic development in African states, this new African conception of the future of Africa lays claim not only to a future, but also to deep roots in the past. President Kaunda insists on this:

> The traditional community was a mutual aid society. It was organized to satisfy the basic human needs of all its members and, therefore, individualism was discouraged. Most resources, such as land, might be communally owned and administered by chiefs and village headmen for the benefit of everyone. If, for example, a villager required a new hut, all the men would turn to forests and fetch poles to erect the frame and bring grass for thatching. The women might be re-

sponsible for making the mud-plaster for the walls
and two or three of them would undoubtedly brew
some beer so that all the workers would be refreshed
after a hot but satisfying day's work. In the same spirit,
the able-bodied would accept responsibility for tend-
ing and harvesting the gardens of the sick and infirm.

This new recognition so characteristic first of Tanzania and
now of Zambia does not turn its back on the modernization necessary in the modern world. Once more let the African President
speak: from what has been said above, it is clear that we cannot
ourselves expect to achieve once again the Man-centered society
without very careful planning. And in this direction nothing is
more important than institutions of learning.

Here the model is or will have to be that so clearly deline-
ated by Dr. Nyerere. That is the essence of the matter. And the
newly independent African states are in such crises that success
in Tanzania and real strides forward in hard-pressed Zambia can
initiate a new road for Africa—the mobilization of the African
people to build an African society in an African way.

It would be a great mistake not to make clear how reality corresponds with—and indeed carries further—the highest stages so far reached by Western political thought. Lenin
had no illusions about the Russian Revolution. He knew that
socialism in the Marxist sense was impossible in the Russia he
knew, and in 1923 was leaving behind. In the last days he increasingly drew attention to two important aspects and needs
of the Russia which he insisted on calling Socialist Russia, despite the fact that the great majority of the Russian population
consisted of illiterate peasants. The Soviet State, he insisted
in those last days, was not new. Behind the Marxist terminol-
ogy and proletarian window dressing was the same old Czarist
state, not even a bourgeois state but a "bureaucratic-serf state."
His proposals to alter these we need not go into. It is sufficient
to know that Dr. Nyerere has seen through the reactionary, bureaucratic colonialist state which he inherited, and has gone
further than anyone in the determination to break it up and
make a new type of state.

Lenin also knew, none better, that the Soviet official had to leave high-flown theorizing and personally go to work among the backward Russian peasants. In perhaps the most moving of his many statements of what the people needed from the Marxist officials of the Government, he says:

> Less argument about words! We still have too much of this sort of thing. More variety in practical experience and more study of this experience! Under certain conditions the exemplary organization of local work, even on a small scale, is of far greater national importance than many branches of the central state work. And these are precisely the conditions we are in at the present moment in regard to peasant farming in general, and in regard to the exchange of the surplus products of agriculture for the manufactures of industry in particular. Exemplary organization in this respect, even in a single *volost*, is of far greater national importance than the "exemplary" improvement of the central apparatus of any People's Commissariat; for three and a half years to such an extent that it has managed to acquire a certain amount of harmful inertness; we cannot improve it quickly to any extent, we do not know how to do it. Assistance in the more radical improvement of it, a new flow of fresh forces, assistance in the successful struggle against bureaucracy, in the struggle to overcome this harmful inertness, must come from the localities, from the lower ranks, with the exemplary organization of a small "whole," precisely a "whole," i.e. not one farm, not one branch of economy, not one enterprise, but the *sum total* of economic exchange, even if only in a small locality.
>
> Those of us who are doomed to remain on work at the center will continue the task of improving the apparatus and purging it of bureaucracy, even if in modest and immediately achievable dimensions. But the greatest assistance in this task is coming, and will come, from the localities.

Note in particular one of his last sentences: "We who are doomed." Lenin wanted to go and work among the peasants. The great Marxist would have understood the profoundly socialist and human conception which has moved Dr. Nyerere to break to pieces the old system of education and substitute a genuinely socialist and humanist procedure for the youth of Tanzania. In a conversation with Dr. Nyerere, the present writer (having previously read his writings) drew his attention to this particular passage from Lenin and what Lenin was striving to teach as far back as 1923. The African leader said that he did not know it—he had arrived at his conclusion by himself and with his people.

It is sufficient to say that socialist thought has seen nothing like this since the death of Lenin in 1924, and its depth, range and the repercussions which flow from it, go far beyond the Africa which gave it birth. It can fertilize and reawaken the mortuary that is socialist theory and practice in the advanced countries. "Marxism is a Humanism" is the exact reverse of the truth. The African builders of a humanist society show that today all humanism finds itself in close harmony with the original conceptions and aims of Marxism.

PM Press was founded at the end of 2007 by a small collection of folks with decades of publishing, media, and organizing experience. PM Press co-conspirators have published and distributed hundreds of books, pamphlets, CDs, and DVDs. Members of PM have founded enduring book fairs, spearheaded victorious tenant organizing campaigns, and worked closely with bookstores, academic conferences, and even rock bands to deliver political and challenging ideas to all walks of life. We're old enough to know what we're doing and young enough to know what's at stake.

We seek to create radical and stimulating fiction and non-fiction books, pamphlets, t-shirts, visual and audio materials to entertain, educate and inspire you. We aim to distribute these through every available channel with every available technology—whether that means you are seeing anarchist classics at our bookfair stalls; reading our latest vegan cookbook at the café; downloading geeky fiction e-books; or digging new music and timely videos from our website.

PM Press is always on the lookout for talented and skilled volunteers, artists, activists and writers to work with. If you have a great idea for a project or can contribute in some way, please get in touch.

PM Press
PO Box 23912
Oakland CA 94623
510-658-3906
www.pmpress.org

These are indisputably momentous times—the financial system is melting down globally and the Empire is stumbling. Now more than ever there is a vital need for radical ideas.

In the four years since its founding—and on a mere shoestring—PM Press has risen to the formidable challenge of publishing and distributing knowledge and entertainment for the struggles ahead. With over 200 releases to date, we have published an impressive and stimulating array of literature, art, music, politics, and culture. Using every available medium, we've succeeded in connecting those hungry for ideas and information to those putting them into practice.

Friends of PM allows you to directly help impact, amplify, and revitalize the discourse and actions of radical writers, filmmakers, and artists. It provides us with a stable foundation from which we can build upon our early successes and provides a much-needed subsidy for the materials that can't necessarily pay their own way. You can help make that happen —and receive every new title automatically delivered to your door once a month—by joining as a Friend of PM Press. And, we'll throw in a free T-Shirt when you sign up.

Here are your options:

- $25 a month: Get all books and pamphlets plus 50% discount on all webstore purchases

- $40 a month: Get all PM Press releases (including CDs and DVDs) plus 50% discount on all webstore purchases

- $100 a month: Superstar—Everything plus PM merchandise, free downloads, and 50% discount on all webstore purchases

For those who can't afford $25 or more a month, we're introducing Sustainer Rates at $15, $10 and $5. Sustainers get a free PM Press t-shirt and a 50% discount on all purchases from our website.

Your Visa or Mastercard will be billed once a month, until you tell us to stop. Or until our efforts succeed in bringing the revolution around. Or the financial meltdown of Capital makes plastic redundant. Whichever comes first.

The Charles H. Kerr Library

ALSO AVAILABLE FROM PM PRESS

State Capitalism and World Revolution
by C.L.R. James,
Raya Dunayevskaya,
and Grace Lee Boggs
ISBN: 978-1-60486-092-4
$16.95

Sixty years ago, C.L.R. James and a small circle of collaborators set forth a revolutionary critique of industrial civilization. Their vision possessed a striking originality. So insular was the political context of their theoretical breakthroughs, however, and so thoroughly did their optimistic expectations for working class activity defy trends away from class and social issues to the so-called 'End of Ideology,' that the documents of the signal effort never reached public view. Happily, times have changed. Readers have discovered much, even after all these years, to challenge Marxist (or any other) orthodoxy. They will never find a more succinct version of James' general conclusions than State Capitalism and World Revolution. In this slim volume, James and his comrades successfully predict the future course of Marxism.

Written in collaboration with Raya Dunayevskaya and Grace Lee Boggs, this is another pioneering critique of Lenin and Trotsky, and reclamation of Marx, from the West Indian scholar and activist, C.L.R. James. Originally published in 1950, this edition includes the original preface from Martin Glaberman, and a new introduction from Paul Buhle.

Praise:

"When one looks back over the last twenty years to those men who were most far-sighted, who first began to tease out the muddle of ideology in our times, who were at the same time Marxists with a hard theoretical basis, and close students of society, humanists with a tremendous response to and understanding of human culture, Comrade James is one of the first one thinks of."—E.P. Thompson

A New Notion: Two Works by C.L.R. James: "Every Cook Can Govern" and "The Invading Socialist Society"
by C.L.R. James
Edited by Noel Ignatiev
ISBN: 978-1-60486-047-4
$16.95

C.L.R. James was a leading figure in the independence movement in the West Indies, and the black and working-class movements in both Britain and the United States. As a major contributor to Marxist and revolutionary theory, his project was to discover, document, and elaborate the aspects of working-class activity that constitute the revolution in today's world. In this volume, Noel Ignatiev, author of *How the Irish Became White*, provides an extensive introduction to James' life and thought, before presenting two critical works that together illustrate the tremendous breadth and depth of James' worldview.

"The Invading Socialist Society," for James the fundamental document of his political tendency, shows clearly the power of James' political acumen and its relevance in today's world with a clarity of analysis that anticipated future events to a remarkable extent. "Every Cook Can Govern," is a short and eminently readable piece counterposing direct with representative democracy, and getting to the heart of how we should relate to one another. Together these two works represent the principal themes that run through James's life: implacable hostility toward all "condescending saviors" of the working class, and undying faith in the power of ordinary people to build a new world.

Praise:

"C.L.R. James has arguably had a greater influence on the underlying thinking of independence movements in the West Indies and Africa than any living man."—*Sunday Times*

"It remains remarkable how far ahead of his time he was on so many issues."—*New Society*

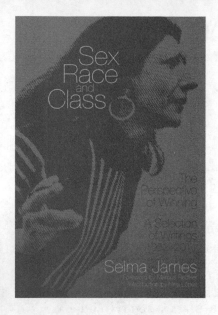

ALSO AVAILABLE FROM PM PRESS & COMMON NOTIONS

Sex, Race, and Class—The Perspective of Winning: A Selection of Writings 1952-2011
by Selma James
ISBN: 978-1-60486-454-0
$20.00

In 1972 Selma James set out a new political perspective. Her starting point was the millions of unwaged women who, working in the home and on the land, were not seen as "workers" and their struggles viewed as outside of the class struggle. Based on her political training in the Johnson-Forest Tendency, founded by her late husband C.L.R. James, on movement experience South and North, and on a respectful study of Marx, she redefined the working class to include sectors previously dismissed as "marginal."

For James, the class struggle presents itself as the conflict between the reproduction and survival of the human race, and the domination of the market with its exploitation, wars, and ecological devastation. She sums up her strategy for change as "Invest in Caring not Killing."

This selection, spanning six decades, traces the development of this perspective in the course of building an international campaigning network. It includes the classic *The Power of Women and the Subversion of the Community* which launched the "domestic labor debate," the exciting *Hookers in the House of the Lord* which describes a church occupation by sex workers, an incisive review of the C.L.R. James masterpiece *The Black Jacobins*, a reappraisal of the novels of Jean Rhys and of the leadership of Julius Nyerere, the groundbreaking *Marx and Feminism*, and more.

The writing is lucid and without jargon. The ideas, never abstract, spring from the experience of organising, from trying to make sense of the successes and the setbacks, and from the need to find a way forward.

ALSO AVAILABLE FROM PM PRESS

Rebel Voices: An IWW Anthology
Edited by Joyce L. Kornbluh
ISBN: 978-1-60486-483-0
$27.95

Welcoming women, blacks, and immigrants long before most other unions, the Wobblies from the start were labor's outstanding pioneers and innovators, unionizing hundreds of thousands of workers previously regarded as "unorganizable." Wobblies organized the first sit-down strike (at General Electric, Schenectady, 1906), the first major auto strike (6,000 Studebaker workers, Detroit, 1911), the first strike to shut down all three coalfields in Colorado (1927), and the first "no-fare" transit-workers' job-action (Cleveland, 1944). With their imaginative, colorful, and world-famous strikes and free-speech fights, the IWW wrote many of the brightest pages in the annals of working class emancipation.

Wobblies also made immense and invaluable contributions to workers' culture. All but a few of America's most popular labor songs are Wobbly songs. IWW cartoons have long been recognized as labor's finest and funniest.

The impact of the IWW has reverberated far beyond the ranks of organized labor. An important influence on the 1960s New Left, the Wobbly theory and practice of direct action, solidarity, and "class-war" humor have inspired several generations of civil rights and antiwar activists, and are a major source of ideas and inspiration for today's radicals. Indeed, virtually every movement seeking to "make this planet a good place to live" (to quote an old Wobbly slogan), has drawn on the IWW's incomparable experience.

Originally published in 1964 and long out of print, *Rebel Voices* remains by far the biggest and best source on IWW history, fiction, songs, art, and lore. This new edition includes 40 pages of additional material from the 1998 Charles H. Kerr edition from Fred Thompson and Franklin Rosemont, and a new preface by Wobbly organizer Daniel Gross.

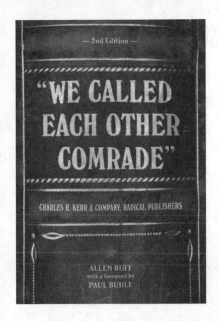

ALSO AVAILABLE FROM PM PRESS

All Power to the Councils!:
A Documentary History of the
German Revolution of 1918–1919
Edited and Translated
by Gabriel Kuhn
ISBN: 978-1-60486-111-2
$26.95

The German Revolution erupted out of the ashes of World War I, triggered by mutinying sailors refusing to be sacrificed in the final carnage of the war. While the Social Democrats grabbed power, radicals across the country rallied to establish a communist society under the slogan "All Power to the Councils!" The Spartacus League launched an uprising in Berlin, council republics were proclaimed in Bremen and Bavaria, and workers' revolts shook numerous German towns. Yet in an act that would tragically shape the course of history, the Social Democratic government crushed the rebellions with the help of right-wing militias, paving the way for the ill-fated Weimar Republic—and ultimately the ascension of the Nazis.

This definitive documentary history collects manifestos, speeches, articles, and letters from the German Revolution—Rosa Luxemburg, the Revolutionary Stewards, and Gustav Landauer amongst others—introduced and annotated by the editor. Many documents, such as the anarchist Erich Mühsam's comprehensive account of the Bavarian Council Republic, are presented here in English for the first time. The volume also includes materials from the Red Ruhr Army that repelled the reactionary Kapp Putsch in 1920 and the communist bandits that roamed Eastern Germany until 1921. *All Power to the Councils!* provides a dynamic and vivid picture of a time of great hope and devastating betrayal.

Praise:

"Gabriel Kuhn's excellent volume illuminates a profound global revolutionary moment, in which brilliant ideas and debates lit the sky."—Marcus Rediker, author of *Villains of all Nations and The Slave Ship*

The Housing Monster

prole.info

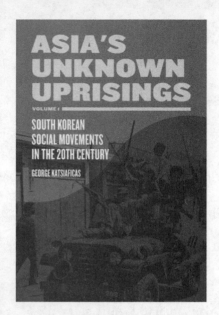